A VOICE SAID AVE!

by

Father Charles Dollen

Mariology is both a science and a devotion. Its roots lie deep in the theology of the Incarnation and in the life of the Mystical Body.

A VOICE SAID AVE! is a devotional tour of the science that teaches us to love the holy Mother of God. This little volume examines selected passages from the writings of the Fathers, Doctors, and theologians as they turned their keen minds to describe Our Lady.

In this book St. Bernard shows us the heights to which we can ascend when we go to Christ, hand in hand with His Blessed Mother. St. Ambrose and St. Augustine indicate the speculative depths that are opened to us when we follow Our Lady.

St. Charles reminds us of the importance of even the most commonplace Marian devotions. St. Thomas Aquinas uses his razor-sharp reasoning on Mary's place in our redemption. In fact, every age of the Church invites us strengthen our love for the little Jewish girl whom God loved first!

A VOICE SAID AVE!

A Voice Said

AVE!

SELECTED PASSAGES ON
OUR LADY FROM THE
WRITINGS OF THE
FATHERS, DOCTORS
AND THEOLOGIANS

FREE TRANSLATIONS BY

FATHER CHARLES DOLLEN

Library Director
University of San Diego

ST. PAUL EDITIONS

NIHIL OBSTAT:

VERY REV. JOHN QUINN
Censor Delegatus

IMPRIMATUR:

MOST REV. CHARLES FRANCIS BUDDY, PH.D.
Bishop of San Diego

January 12, 1963

Library of Congress Catalog Card Number: 63-18346

Printed in U.S.A. by the *Daughters of St. Paul*
50 St. Paul's Ave., Jamaica Plain, Boston 30, Mass.

FOR

CECILIA

CONTENTS

3: *Blessed Is the Fruit of Your Womb* 67

4: *Holy Mary, Mother of God* 89

5: *Pray for Us, Sinners* 111

6: *Madonna* 137

A Voice Said Ave!

The Archangel Gabriel saluted a little Jewish maiden, and his "Ave!" hailed the beginning of the eternal drama of our economy of salvation. The decree that went forth from Caesar Augustus with all its pomp and splendor was a vague shadow or a distant echo, compared with the Almighty decree from the Holy Trinity sending the Archangel with his greeting.

Who would ever remember that Imperial edict if it had not had a place in the Divine Plan? Not all the force of Caesar's Rome would ever affect mankind as did the consequences flowing from that simple "Ave!"

The centuries, the millenia, of preparation for the Incarnation were clues to what the fullness of time would bring forth. Central to God's plan was a woman, His own choice, the one who would give to Christ all His human heredity, characteristics and talents.

Eve, Sara, Rebecca, Rachel, Esther, Judith and all the holy women of the Old Testament pointed to Mary. Whatever the role that these individual women played in their own time, their importance in leading to Jesus through Mary cannot be overemphasized.

Almost as soon as the Church had the peace it needed for external organization, Christian writers began exploring the depths of the deposit of Faith. With all the dynamic challenge this provided, through subsequent years of fighting heresy, while promoting the growth of the Christ-life in those who sought perfection, in all of these, the role of Mary was just naturally treated.

The earliest writers felt that Christianity was inextricably permeated with Mary. Christ came into the world physically in one age, through Mary; He continues to come, theologically and spiritually, in every age, through Mary. Inevitably, Christian writers were soon producing works specifically Marian in character.

But, was devotion to the Blessed Virgin Mary simply a "medieval accretion" to the body of Catholic Faith? Emphatically, no! In the pages that follow, the tribute of the centuries is seen, the love of Mary that comes from the hearts and pens of the Fathers, Doctors, Saints, and writers of every age.

The universality of this devotion is, in itself, a wonder. The mere antiquity of some of the passages might be interesting, although it would prove little. But the complete coverage, the whole voice of a living tradition, great saints and writers of East and West—this entire unanimity is witness to a great truth. Love of Mary is a mark of those who know, love, adore and serve Christ.

We have come to expect great effusions of love for Mary from St. Bernard, "the troubadour of Mary" and the last of the Fathers. We expect to see great basilicas in the thirteenth century dedicated to the holy Mother of God. But the words of the centuries before and after are just as extravagant as anything that Bernard wrote. Marian shrines, in word and work, are to be found wherever there is love for Jesus Christ, her Son.

In the great desire now prevalent for Christian unity, some have suggested that the Catholic devotion to the Blessed Virgin may prove an obstacle too great to surmount. This cannot be. Wherever the Catholic spirit flourishes, there is devotion to the Mother of God. Without it we cannot recognize the Church of the Ages, the Church of Christ. Love and devotion for Mary could, under the inspiration of the Holy Spirit, be the bridge to unite all things again in Christ.

"To Jesus through Mary" is the joyful cry of all the Christian ages.

* * *

The translations presented here are taken from two sources. Most passages are taken from the Roman Breviary where they are (or were) used as lessons for various feasts, principally those of Our Lady. The longer selections from St. Thomas Aquinas, St. Charles Borromeo, and Suarez are translations from volumes preserved in the rare book collection of the University of San Diego Library.

Wherever possible, "you" has been substituted for "thou" as being more in keeping with the character of a free translation. In this spirit, the following chapters are presented as a work of devotion, not as a scholarly treatise on Mariology.

F. Nagni

Hail magnificent edifice, most holy, pure and immaculate. O Palace of the most high King, infused with the magnificence of the Divine King Himself, receiving all who come with love, refreshing all with spiritual delights.

St. Germanus

Chapter 1

Hail, Full of Grace!

Now in the sixth month
the angel Gabriel was sent
from God to a town of Galilee
called Nazareth, to a virgin
betrothed to a man named Joseph,
of the house of David,
and the virgin's name was Mary.
And when the angel had come
to her, he said,
"Hail, full of grace,
the Lord is with thee.
Blessed art thou among women."
When she had heard him
she was troubled at his word,
and kept pondering
what manner of greeting
this might be.
And the angel said to her,
"Do not be afraid, Mary,
for thou hast found
grace with God."

Luke 1:26-30.

The Fathers and Doctors of the Church have found an inexhaustible source of material in this passage. They have taken every phrase of it and speculated, meditated, and contemplated, upon the mysterious depths it contains.

The following passages are typical of the various ways it has been treated. Throughout all of them, the happiness, the wonder, the source of Christian hope are evident.

The difference of approach is interesting to watch, as well as the use of the Scriptures. Whatever the beauty of thought, however extravagant the praise, underlying every approach is the relationship of Jesus and Mary, the basic reason why Mary is so honored.

The prophecy "All generations shall call me blessed" is amply fulfilled here. If the angels could hardly restrain themselves, it is no wonder that man cannot remain silent. Neither is it any wonder that Pope John XXIII, in a MOTU PROPRIO *in* 1960, *urged us to investigate the riches to be found in the writings of these great men.*

ST. JEROME:

Sermon on the Assumption

When the Angel cried "Hail, full of Grace, the Lord is with you; you are blessed among women!" he told us by Divine command how tremendous was the dignity and beauty of the ever-virgin Mary. How well we can understand that she would be "full of Grace," this Virgin who glorified God and gave Our Lord to mankind, who poured out peace upon the earth by giving hope to the Gentiles, protection against temptation, purpose to life and reason for sacrifice.

Others may grow in grace, day by day, but in Mary there has been poured the fullness of Grace. Although we may know that the holy Patriarchs and Prophets had Grace, it was much different from the fullness of Grace found in Mary, the fullness of the Grace of Christ.

When we read "You are blessed among women" we understand "You are more blessed than any woman ever created." Whatever penalty was decreed against Eve is totally removed in the blessing poured forth in Mary.

Solomon sings her praises in his Canticles— "Come my dove, immaculate one, for winter is over, the rains have come and gone."And again, "Come from Lebanon, come and be crowned."

Fittingly she is called forth from Lebanon, for Lebanon means "snow-white". By the merits of her many virtues, by the gifts of the Holy Spirit, Mary has been adorned and cleansed, whiter than any snow. She has the simplicity of the dove in all things. All purity and simplicity are found in her, all truth and grace, all the mercy and the justice showered down from Heaven. She is truly immaculate, for no stain is found in her.

Jeremias affirms that she carried a man in her womb without physical contact. He tells us that the Lord has done something unique on the earth when this woman shall bear a man. It is so truly unique that it can have no equal. God, whom the whole world cannot contain, nor any man see and still live, God has found a welcome in her womb. Without injuring her physical virginity, the whole God enters in, and likewise, is born, although, as Ezechiel testifies, the door remained entirely closed.

Solomon goes on in his Canticle, "an enclosed garden, a sealed fountain, your flowers a Paradise." What a garden of delights in which are found all the the blossoms and scent of all the virtues! This garden is so protected that no evil or corruption can enter. This fountain is surely sealed with the mark of the whole Trinity.

ST. GERMANUS:

Homily on the Presentation of the Mother of God

Hail, Mary, full of Grace, more saintly than any of the other saints, higher than the highest heavens, more dazzling than the Cherubim, lovelier than the Seraphim, most honored of all creation. Hail, O Dove, bringing us the olive branch and the glad news of a Savior from the spiritual deluge, a harbor of safety. Hail, O Dove, whose bright wings and golden hue reflect the splendor of the Holy Spirit.

Hail, O Paradise of every rational delight, firmly established by the right hand of God, extending from East to West the sweet fragrance of the lily and the refreshing scent of the rose to strengthen those immersed in spiritual despair and death. O Paradise in which the love of truth flourishes, and the tree of life, the source of eternal life for those who taste.

Hail magnificent edifice, most holy, pure and immaculate. O Palace of the most high King, infused with the magnificence of the Divine King Himself, receiving all who come with love, refreshing all with spiritual delights. In you the mystical Bridegroom found repose on a couch of beauty, not made with hands; in you the Word took flesh that

He might bring back the erring race which had exiled itself, and restore it to the Father.

Hail Mountain of God, rich and restful, pasture of the Lamb who bore our sins and infirmities. O Mountain from which that stone comes, not hewn by hand, to crush the altars of idols, that stone which has become the head of the corner, so marvelous in in our eyes.

Hail holy Throne of God, Divine Tabernacle, House of Glory, precious Jewel, Haven of Mercy for all the world, declaring the glories of the God of Heaven. Hail golden Urn containing Christ, the manna of our souls, the source of all refreshment.

O Virgin most pure and worthy of all praise, sanctuary consecrated above all mankind, field unploughed, virgin land, flourishing vine, living fountain. O fruitful Virgin, untouched by man, delicate treasure of innocence and holiness!

Direct all members of the Church to their safe harbor by your motherly love and intercession, so acceptable to your Son, the Lord and God of all creation, born from you without human father.

Pour out justice upon the priesthood; clothe priests with the joy of a living faith, strong, spotless and sincere. Direct the hand of Catholic princes in the rule of their kingdoms since they have their love and faith in you, as jewels more precious than their earthly treasure.

ST. SOPHRONIUS:

Homily on the Annunciation to the Mother of God

What does that blessed spirit say when he is sent to a virgin so perfectly endowed with integrity? How does he present this, the happiest message of all time? "Hail, full of Grace, the Lord is with you."

Joyfully he brings her the message of joy. How well he realizes that his is an announcement of joy for all men, for all creatures, that it will mean the end of sorrow for all. He knows that the world will glow with the radiance of this divine mystery. He understands full well that the mists of error, the pangs of death, the power of corruption and the forces of hell will fall back before the light of salvation rising over mankind. Too long has mankind, expelled from paradise, cast out from home, been oppressed by the yoke of these evils.

Therefore, the angel begins his mission with joy. His joyful greeting initiates the message of happiness that will extend to all the faithful. Therefore, indeed, the divine message of joy begins with words that elicit joy. Since the angel was not ignorant of the import of his joyful mission, he emphasizes the note of joy that will pour unceasingly on the world.

And indeed, can any joy or rapture be discovered that is not far surpassed by the meaning of this greeting to the Blessed Virgin, the Mother of Joy? Rejoice, O Mother of Heavenly Joy!

Rejoice, O Mother of sublime joy. Rejoice, O Mother of immortal joy. Rejoice, O Throne of salutary joy, mystical home of ineffable joy, blessed fountain of unending joy, rejoice! Rejoice, O God-bearing treasure-house of eternal joy, ever-flourishing tree of life-giving joy. Virgin before and after childbirth, rejoice! Mother of God, wonder of wonders, rejoice!

Who can describe your splendor or dare to enumerate your glories? Who would feel capable of depicting your magnificence?

You have adored human nature and been exalted above all the orders of angels. You have overshadowed the archangels, seen the sublime seats of the Thrones below you, and even the loftiness of the Dominations. You outrank the Principalities, have strength beyond the Powers, and outstrip the Virtues in excellence. Your earthly eyes see more than a Cherub's bright glance; your soul soars higher with Divine guidance than the six-winged Seraphim.

You have been raised above every creature. You have surpassed all in purity. Only you have been chosen to bear the Creator of all creatures in your womb, given Him to the world, pressed Him to your bosom.

Only you, from among all creation, have been made the Mother of God.

ST. THARASIUS:

On the Presentation of the Mother of God

O Mary, how can I add to your praises? O virgin undefiled, virgin immaculate, glory of mothers, splendor of daughters! O holy Virgin Mother, you are blessed among all women, praised for your innocence, your virginity.

Adam's curse ceases with you; Eve's debt is repaid. You are Abel's pleasing sacrifice, an oblation clean and pure. In you, Enoch's hope and trust in God is secured, his transition to glory assured. You are the Ark of Noah and the reconciliation between God and man.

Melchisedech's royal priesthood shines forth in you, as well as Abraham's faith, so fruitful in promise. You are the new sacrifice of Isaac, the pleasing burnt-offering. You are Jacob's vision of the heavenly ladder, the noblest offspring of all his twelve children.

Daughter of Judah according to the flesh, the virtue of Joseph abounds in you. O Immaculate one, the destruction of Egypt was accomplished in you, and the victory over the opposition of the Jewish synagogue. You are Moses and the Book of the Law, expounding the mysteries of salvation. You are the divinely written Tables of the Law, given from Mt. Sinai.

The deliverance of the new Israel comes through you. The people of God are fed with the true manna, refreshed with the truly satisfying waters, both types of Christ who was to spring from your womb as a bridegroom from his couch. You are the flowering rod of Aaron, David's glorious daughter, surrounded and clothed with beauty.

You are the mirror of the prophets, the fulfillment of their work. Ezechiel called you the closed gate through which no man has ever passed, save only the Lord God, and He kept the gate closed. Isaias foretold you as the valiant rod of Jesse from which the flower, Christ, would arise to conquer all vice and to plant the fields with virtue.

Jeremias spoke for God when he said that days would come in which the Lord would make a new covenant with the house of Israel and the house of Judah, even as He had with their fathers, signifying the advent of your Son who would call all nations to the worship of God. Daniel, that man of great desires, called you the wonderful mountain from which would come the Christ, the cornerstone, to scatter and destroy the works of the serpent.

Now let me add my poor praises! O Immaculate lamb, O truly full of Grace, O pure and immaculate tabernacle of God! Where sin once abounded, Grace, indeed, has superabounded.

Through a woman came death; through the woman He will restore the whole world. Through the serpent came the food of death; through her we will again taste the food of immortality. Through Eve came Cain, the progenitor of envy and evil; in your only-begotten Son will come the first-fruits of life and resurrection.

O marvel defying words! A novelty above admiration! O wisdom beyond description!

Now we, the people of God, a holy nation, an acceptable generation, progeny of the dove, we, the children of grace come together with uplifted minds and voices to sing the praises of this Virgin on her feast-day. Angels and men unite with joy to repeat Gabriel's noble "Ave!"

Hail, delight of the Father, through whom the knowledge of God is spread through the entire world. Hail, home of the Son, from whom He took flesh. Hail, temple of the Holy Spirit!

Hail Mary—holier than the Cherubim, more glorious than the Seraphim, higher than the heavens, brighter than the sun, lovelier than the moon, fairer than the stars, gentler than the rain clouds and the dew! Hail refreshing breeze, dissipating the mists of evil.

Hail noble herald of the prophets, apostolic voice resounding throughout the whole world. Hail triumphant confession of the martyrs, venerable fulfillment of the patriarchs' visions, adornment of of all the saints!

Hail Mary—cause of our salvation, reigning Queen of Peace, immaculate splendor of motherhood. Hail, mediatrix of all the living, reparatrix of all the world.

Hail, full of Grace, the Lord is with you, He who was before you, from you, and with us. To Him, with the Father and the most holy, life giving Spirit, be given all praise now and forever throughout all the endless ages. Amen.

ST. BERNARD:

First Homily on the Missus Est

Gabriel was not, in my opinion, an angel of one of the lower orders who are so often sent into the world on various matters. I take this from his name, which means, "Strength of God," and from the fact that he was a direct emmisary from God, and not from some higher ranking angel, as might happen. Perhaps this is the reason why the Gospel adds, "from God," or, it could be to show that God did not reveal His plan to anyone before the Virgin, except the archangel Gabriel.

Only Gabriel was found among the archangels to be worthy of the name and the message, between which there is real harmony. Who could better announce the power of God, Christ, than an angel bearing that name? Is not power strength? It is hardly incongruous that Our Lord and His messenger should be designated by the same word. However, what is similar in word is not necessarily similar in origin! Christ is essentially the power, or strength, of God. For the angel it is only a name.

Christ is called, and is, the power of God. He is that conquering hero who overcomes the stronghold of the armed man, and who, by His strength, liberates the captives.

The angel is called the strength of God either as a prerogative of his office, announcing the advent of the Power of God, or because it was his privilege to strengthen the Virgin so that this unique miracle would not frighten her in her natural humility, modesty and simplicity. He certainly did strengthen her when he said, "Do not be afraid, Mary, because you have found grace before God."

It was fitting that Gabriel be chosen for such a work; indeed, because he was to be engaged in so great a mission, it was fitting that so great a name be given to him.

ST. LEO:

Second Sermon on the Nativity of Our Lord

The almighty and merciful God, whose nature is goodness, whose will is power, and whose work is mercy, announced immediately after the diabolical evil that poisoned mankind, the prescribed remedy that would renew the human race. He solemnly warned the serpent that the seed of the woman would come to crush his proud, exulting head, that is, the Christ Who would come in the flesh. Christ, the God-man born of the Virgin, would condemn the violator of the human race by His pure birth.

For the devil was exulting in the deceit he had practiced on man, causing him to lose the divinely given gifts. Man had stripped himself of the gift of immortality and could look forward only to the sentence of death. Perhaps the devil found some comfort in having a partner in crime!

It seemed as if he could force God to change His mind about the human race. God had constituted man a creature of honor, but now the piercing demands of justice would change things.

But, dearly beloved, the unchangeable God, whose will includes all goodness, completed His original intent of love by a yet more mysterious disposition of love. Man, overwhelmed by guilt through an act of diabolical craftiness, would not perish contrary to the plan of God.

Beloved brethren, when the time for man's redemption arrived, Our Lord Jesus Christ came down to our lowly world, came down from His heavenly throne without leaving the paternal beatitude, came in a new order, a new birth. It was a new order because He Who is invisible in His own life became visible in ours. He the incomprehensible willed to be comprehended.

Existing before all time, He willed to enter into the temporal order. The Lord of the universe took upon Himself the form of a servant, covering over the glory of His majesty. As God He was above all suffering, yet He did not hesitate at all to become the suffering servant. Immortal, He subjected Himself to the law of mortality.

ST. PETER CHRYSOLOGUS:

Sermon on the Annunciation

You have heard today, beloved brethren, what an angel said to a woman about the rebirth of mankind. You have heard how man may return to life along the same paths that lead to death. The angel gives Mary the message of salvation even as once an angel had given Eve the message of doom. You have heard from an angel how a temple of divine majesty can be erected from one of our race through a mysterious power.

You have heard the incredible mystery whereby God is placed on earth so that man may be replaced in heaven. Yes, you have heard the tremendous mystery of God joined in one body with man. You have heard how one of our flesh, by angelic encouragement, is fortified to bear the total glory of the God-head.

"Do not be afraid, Mary," the angel says, lest Mary, conscience of the frailty of our nature might hesitate to put the strain of a divine burden on our weak flesh. The Virgin might fear to carry the fruit of the entire human race on such a tender branch. Even before we know the reason, the dignity of this Virgin has been announced by her name.

F. Nagni

"Do not be afraid, Mary, for you have found Grace." How true this is! Whoever finds grace has nothing to fear, and "you have found Grace."

St. Peter Chrysologus

Mary, translated from Hebrew to Latin, means "Lady." The angel calls her "Lady" so that the consciousness of her natural lowliness will not stay her who is to be the Mother of the Lord. On the authority of her Son, it was decreed and effected that she be born and be called "Lady."

"Do not be afraid, Mary, for you have found Grace." How true this is! Whoever finds grace has nothing to fear, and "you have found Grace." O Blessed Virgin who alone merited to hear these words before any others of our race, "you have found Grace."

How much Grace? As was said before, Grace in its fullness. Like a drenching rain Grace has covered and immersed this creature. Even the angel marvels as he says it, "You have found Grace." He stands back, amazed that this woman alone has merited life, and through her, all mankind.

The angel is lost in wonder that the true God enters the confines of the virginal womb—He for whom the entire universe is too small. Therefore, the angel pauses. He calls her rightfully virgin; he acknowledges the gift of Grace within her. Then, almost in fear, the angel seems to plead his case, begging approval.

ST. BERNARD:

Sermon on the Aqueduct

The Word was made flesh and now lives in our midst. He lingers in our memories, He dwells in our thoughts, He even comes down into our imaginations. How, you may ask, does He do this?

He does it by resting in the manger, reposing in His mother's bosom, preaching on the mountainside, keeping vigil throughout the night, hanging on the cross with the pallor of death coming over Him, freely among the dead, conquering Hell.

He continues it in His Resurrection on the third day, in showing the apostles the place of the nails, the signs of His victory, and finally in His Ascension to the highest Heaven before their very eyes!

On which of these actions may we not pause and meditate with truth, love and devotion? When I meditate about any of these facts, I meditate about God! In each of these, He is my God. I call it the mark of wisdom to contemplate these things. I judge it prudent to bring up the memory of their sweetness.

From such seed as this, the priestly rod produced fruit in great measure. Drawing from these sublime fountains, Mary has poured forth upon us the nourishing drink of great profit. She who is on a heavenly plane beyond all the angels had received the Word from the heart of the Father, Himself.

For this is the new day of creation, the day on which the Father gives the light of salvation. But is it not also the Virgin's day, when she approaches bright and shining as the dawn, beautiful as the moon, radiant as the sun!

Truth has finally returned to the earth, not through angelic creatures, nor through any individual angel, but through this daughter of Abraham. Great as the angels are who minister to God, Mary far surpasses them, for she has been chosen not as servant, but as Mother.

For the rest, brethren, let us be mindful that the Word which proceeds from the mouth of the Father, comes to us only through the work of this Virgin. If we were silent about this, our very silence would cry out! If we are faithful in these meditations, know that we will obtain the light of His presence.

ST. AMBROSE:

From the Book of Offices

Modesty is the good friend and guardian of purity. This is immediately evident when we read about the Mother of the Lord. It is a trustworthy testimonial to the fact that she was worthy to be chosen for so great a work.

She was alone in her room when she was saluted by the angel. She was silent to his greeting and disturbed at his entrance. The Virgin was troubled by the unexpected apparition of a strong young man in her room.

In real humility and because of her modesty, the Virgin was silent and did not respond to the angelic salutation until she understood that she was to become the Mother of Our Lord. Then she responded, not to wonder about the message, but only to learn what God's plan entailed for her.

F. Nagni

Truly you are blessed among all women because, while remaining a woman, a creature of our race, you have become the Mother of God.

St. Sophronius

Chapter 2

Blessed Among Women

Now in those days Mary arose and
went with haste into the hill
country, to a town of Juda.
And she entered the house of
Zachary and saluted Elizabeth.
And it came to pass, when Elizabeth
heard the greeting of Mary,
that the babe in her womb leapt.
And Elizabeth was filled
with the Holy Spirit, and cried
out with a loud voice, saying,
"Blessed art thou among women
and blessed is the fruit
of thy womb!
And how have I deserved
that the mother of my Lord
should come to me?"

Luke 1:39-43.

How many ways are there to express most-blessed, or thrice-blessed? What is the superlative of a superlative? As the poetess inferred, can we count or number the ways of love?

The Fathers were not stopped by this seemingly insurmountable problem in semantics. They delighted in the phrase "Blessed art thou among women" and they looked for new and fascinating ways to praise the Virgin who had first been praised by God. God had praised her! That is the one common note in their wonderment. Yet she remained only a simple child of our race, a creature, a woman. In fact, the Fathers loved this idea, too, for it made our claim upon her more forceful.

They did not expect her to "stoop to our level." She was one of us, raised to sublime heights by the work and will of God. The Fathers would never have been surprised by the marvel of Our Lady's work at Guadalupe, for instance. They would expect her to be at ease, as Queen, among nobles, or as Mother to the lowliest victim of social injustice. In our day, they might look for her among the victims of segregation or of "liberation."

Their surprise would be rather that we need visions and apparitions to increase our love of Mary. When God called Mary "blessed," the Fathers understood it as a cry of love, and their magnificent hearts responded promptly.

ST. SOPHRONIUS:

Homily on the Annunciation to the Mother of God

Truly you are blessed among women because you have turned the curse of Eve into a blessing. You have given hope to Adam, prostrate under the weight of the divine decree. You are indeed blessed among women because the blessing of God the Father has come, through you, to mankind, freeing the whole race from the ancient curse.

Truly you are blessed among women because all your forebears have found their salvation through you, since you are to give birth to the Savior Who will open heaven to them. You are indeed blessed among women because without male seed you will produce the fruit which will fill the world with blessings and destroy the weeds of wickedness.

Truly you are blessed among all women because, while remaining a woman, a creature of our race, you have become the Mother of God. For, if the Holy One born of your womb is truly God Incarnate, then must you truly be called the Mother of God, since you have, in absolute truth, brought forth God.

Do not be afraid, Mary, because you have found grace before God, grace unable to be lost, above all measure, exceeding all expectations, more glorious than that ever given to anyone. You have found such grace in God's sight that it will never fail.

You have found grace before God which will be your salvation, which will never be shaken by any force, wholly unconquerable, enduring forever. Indeed, there were others before you, many others, in whom holiness flourished, but never was it granted to anyone to be full of grace, as you are.

No one was ever before raised to such heights of magnificence, as you. No one was ever so immaculately pure, beforehand, as you. Never before was there one who shone so brightly with heavenly light, who was so exalted above all the heavens.

And rightly so, for no one has ever been so close to God as you. On no one has God ever bestowed the gifts He has given to you. No one but you has been so full a participant in God's grace.

You have been placed above every other creature, no matter how great. You have received more gifts than God has ever bestowed in all His goodness on any creature. You have grown richer than all by the possession of God living within you. No one else ever contained God within, as you did!

Never before has a creature grown full with the presence of God. No one has ever been found so worthy as to be thus treated by God. Not only have you received the Lord God, Creator of all, but He took flesh from you in a wondrous manner. He grew in your womb and was born to redeem a race which groaned under His Father's curse, and to offer man unending salvation, pouring Himself out, lavishly.

Therefore I have cried out to you, and will continue to do so, unceasingly, "Hail, full of grace, the Lord is with you; you are blessed among women!"

ST. BERNARD:

First Homily on the Missus Est

And He was subject to them. Who? And to whom? God was subject to man! God, I repeat, to whom the angels are subject, whom Principalities and Powers obey, was subject to Mary, and not only to Mary, but to Joseph, too, because of Mary.

Wonder, indeed, at both, but choose which is the more wonderful. Is it that most living condescension of the Son, or the tremendous dignity of the Mother? Both are astounding; both miraculous.

God submitting in obedience to a woman is indeed humility without equal; the woman commanding her God is sublime beyond measure. In praising virgins we read that they follow the Lamb wherever He goes. How can we possibly praise enough the Virgin who leads Him?

Learn, O man, to obey. Learn, O earth, to be subject. Learn, O dust, to bow down. In speaking of our Creator, the Evangelist says, "And He was subject to them," that is, to Mary and Joseph.

Blush, O proud ashes! God humiliates Himself and you exalt yourselves. God subjected Himself to man, but you, desiring to dominate your fellowman, place yourselves above your Creator. If it

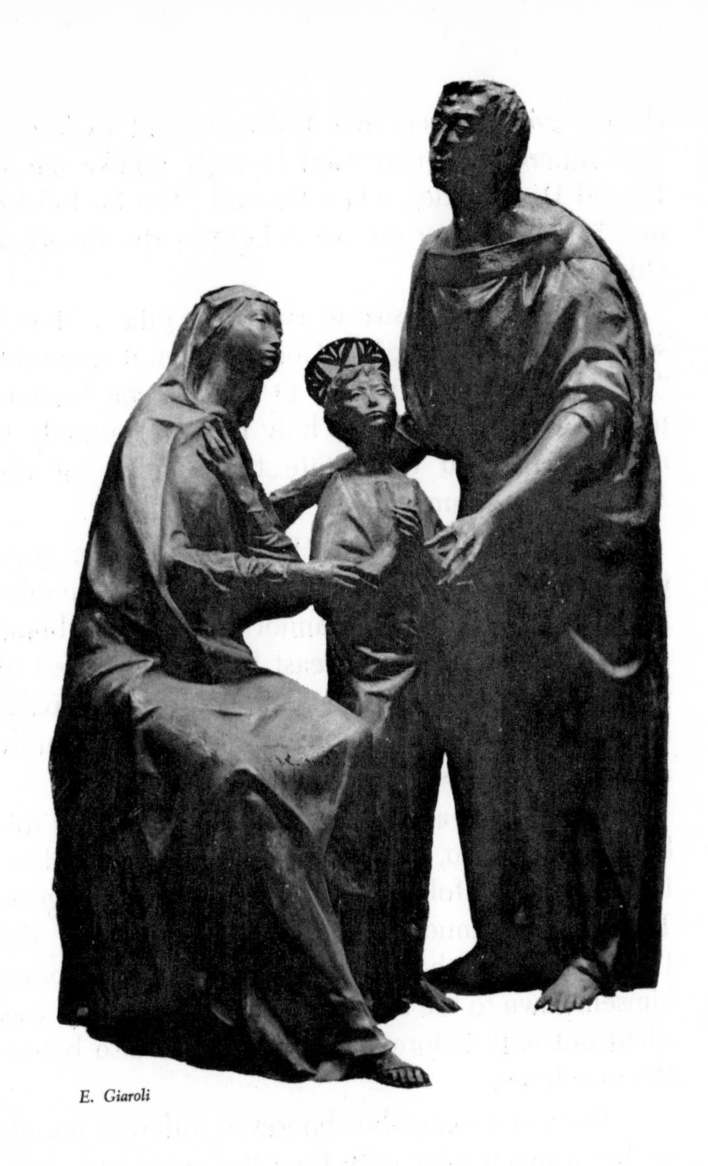

E. Giaroli

God submitting in obedience to a woman is indeed humility without equal; the woman commanding her God is sublime beyond measure.

ST. BERNARD

should ever happen that I would want to lord it over others, then may God lovingly rebuke me as He did His apostles, when He said, "Get far behind me, Satan, for you do not delight in the things of God."

Whenever I desire to rule over others, then I seek to put myself before God. Of Him it was said, "He was subject to them." O man, if you hesitate to follow the example of holy men, it certainly is not beneath you to imitate the example of the Author of the human race.

If you cannot follow Him wherever He goes, then at least deign to follow Him when He humbles Himself for you. If you cannot follow the sublime pathways of virginity, at least follow that safest of pathways, humility. Whoever strays from this path, no matter how virginal he may be, will certainly not follow the Lamb wherever He goes.

Though not a virgin, the humble man may follow the Lamb. So, also, the proud virgin will follow. But neither will follow the Lamb wherever He goes. The former cannot ascend to the purity of the Lamb who is without spot; the latter cannot bring himself down to the meekness of the Lamb who was silent not only before the shearers, but also before His murderers.

The sinful man who chooses to follow in humility has a much safer path than the proud man who tries to follow in virginity. Humble reparation cleanses the former, even as pride spoils the cleanness of the other.

But Mary is truly blessed, for in her neither virginity nor humility are in any way lacking. Hers is a singular virginity which does not fear childbearing, but rather honors it. She is also endowed with the humility equal to this sublime task. Which of these virtues is more admirable, more incomparable?

Yet do not stop long to make this comparison when there is still another to consider. Which is more marvelous—childbearing in a virgin, or integrity in a mother? God, Who is truly wonderful in His saints, has yet surpassed all wonders in raising His Mother to such sublime heights! O all you angels and saints, honor the Mother of the King you adore, for He made Himself subject to her.

ST. BERNARD:

Second Homily on the Missus Est

It is written: Her husband, Joseph, since he was a just man, unwilling that she be harmed, wanted to send her away secretly. Since he was a just man, he certainly did not want to subject her to reproach. He would not have been a just man if he even seemed to consent to what he knew was sinful; he would certainly have been less than just if he allowed innocence to be condemned.

Therefore, being a just man and unwilling to let her suffer, he wanted to dismiss her quietly. Why did he want to put her away? Take the answers of the Fathers, rather than my opinion.

Joseph wanted her out of his life for the same reason that St. Peter begged Our Lord, "Depart from me, O Lord, for I am a sinful man." It was the same reason the centurion used in discouraging Our Lord from coming to his home, "O Lord, I am not worthy that you should come down under my roof."

Just so, St. Joseph considered himself an unworthy sinner, and he felt deep inside that he should not force his friendship on so great a woman in such a marvelous and mysterious matter. He understood and drew back in awe at these definite traces of the Divine presence. Since he could not penetrate the mystery, he thought rather of sending her away.

Peter was shaken by the magnitude of power. The centurion was awed by the majesty of the Divine presence. So also, Joseph, being only human, trembled in the face of such a unique miracle.

Do you wonder that Joseph judged himself unworthy to be the spouse of this pregnant Virgin when you realize how Elizabeth welcomed her holy presence with a trembling reverence? For Elizabeth cried out, "How can it be that the Mother of my Lord should come to me?"

Therefore, indeed, Joseph wanted to send her away. But why secretly and not openly? If it were done openly, then the reason for the dismissal would have to be explained openly. What reason could a just man give to a stiff-necked people, skeptical and contradictory as they were?

If he said what he believed, and what he knew of her proven purity, would not these unbelieving and harsh countryfolk sneer at him, and stone her? How could they be expected to give credence to Truth itself, silent in her womb, when later they cried out contemptuously at Him as He preached in the temple? What would they have done before

His appearance when later they cruelly seized Him after they had seen His miracles?

No wonder this just man wished to send her away silently, so that he would not have to lie nor seem to defame so innocent a woman.

Even while he was thinking over these things, God mercifully sent an angel to calm his anxiety. "Joseph, son of David, do not fear to take Mary for your wife," was the message delivered while he slept. Only then did this strong, chaste descendant of David take Mary, a virgin of the house of David, for his wife. The oath which God had sworn to David, their father, was to be fulfilled in Mary, while Joseph was the honest, manly witness to the truth of that fulfillment.

ST. AMBROSE:

Second Book on Luke

The divine mysteries are indeed hidden, nor are they easy for anyone (according to the prophetic word) who tries to penetrate the counsel of God. However, from certain facts, and from the deeds of of Our Lord and Savior, we are able to know and to come a little closer to that divine plan which chose directly that she who was to bear Our Lord would be espoused to a man.

Why was that plan not begun before she was espoused? Perhaps so that it could not be said that she had conceived in adultery.

And the angel came to her in whom we discern virginity in manner, modesty, word, and virtue. We expect a true virgin to be modest, to avoid friendship with men, and to be careful of conversation with them. Let all young women learn to profit by this example of modesty.

Only an angel might approach this chamber which was open to no man's view. There alone, without companions or witnesses, with no one to distract her by vain conversation, there she was saluted by the angel.

Only an angel, no mere man, could bring a message so full of mysterious import. For the first time these words are heard, "The Holy Spirit shall come upon you." They are heard and believed. And then her reply, "Behold the handmaiden of the Lord. Be it done to me according to your word."

See the humility! Note well the devotion. She who has been chosen to be the Mother of the Lord calls herself His little servant-girl. She certainly does not become haughty over this promise of so exalted a position. By calling herself a handmaiden she does not take as a right what is freely given as a grace.

ST. JOHN DAMASCENE:

On the True Faith

Joachim was married to Ann, an excellent woman, most worthy of praise. Like that former Anna of ancient times, who, though sterile, received Samuel as an answer to her prayers and vows, so this noble woman, through her prayers and vows received from God the privilege of bearing the Mother of God. Thus, Ann is outstanding among all the illustrious matrons.

And so grace (which is what the name Ann means) brings forth Our Lady (which is the meaning of the name Mary). Certainly Mary is the Lady ruling over all created things, since she is the Mother of the Creator.

Mary was born in Joachim's house, near the pool Probatica, and from there she was brought into the Temple. Then, established in the house of God, strengthened by the Holy Spirit, like a fruitful olive branch, she brought forth all of the virtues worthy of the household of God.

The desires of the world and the concupiscence of the flesh never touched her pure soul. She was preserved virginal body and soul, as became one who would someday receive her God into her bosom.

ST. BASIL:

Commentary on Isaias, the Prophet

I went into the prophetess, he says, and she conceived and gave birth to a son. That Mary was the Prophetess to whom Isaias drew near in spirit, is clear to those who remember Mary's words which she spoke under the influence of a prophetic spirit.

Her words? "My soul magnifies the Lord, and my spirit exults in God, my Savior, because He has taken notice of me, His handmaiden. From now on, every generation shall call me blessed."

If we listen carefully to these words, we cannot deny that she was a Prophetess. The Spirit of the Lord had come upon her and the power of the Most High God had overshadowed her.

ST. JOHN DAMASCENE:

Second Sermon on the Nativity of Mary

Let us propose to ourselves the home of Ann in which we have the example of married bliss in the mother and virginity in the daughter. The mother has but recently been freed from sterility; the daughter will, in a little while, bring forth a child in a manner far above our human condition, through divine intervention.

Therefore, Ann might well cry out, influenced by the Holy Spirit, and overcome with her own happiness, "Come, join in my exultation, for I have brought forth the fruit of promise from my sterile womb and nursed the child of blessedness at my breasts, in fulfillment of my prayers. I have cast aside the sadness of barrenness and been clothed in the joyful garments of fruitfulness.

"Rejoice with me today, Anna, competitor of Phenenna. Celebrate with me this new and longed-for miracle, that I, too, after your example, have given birth to a child. Exult with me, Sara, for your joyful deliverance in your sterile years prefigured mine.

"Let all the barren and sterile sing with me at my wondrous visitation, so divinely fruitful. Let all mothers, too, blessed in my fruitfulness, say 'Blessed is He Who answered the prayers of your longing and gave the child to the childless, Who granted that from this virginal offspring would come God Incarnate. Her womb would be heaven for Him to inhabit, whom the whole heavens cannot contain.' "

We also must join in this song to praise her, once called barren, but now the mother of a Virgin Mother. Let us say to her, with the Scriptures, "How blessed is the house of David which produced you and the womb in which God made the Ark of holiness, that is, the woman from whom He would be conceived without male seed."

O blessed and thrice-blessed Ann, that you have brought forth as a divine gift the infant Mary, honored even in name. From her came Christ, the summit of life. Glorious by birth, this Virgin is raised above all the earth by the Son she will bear.

Ann, blessed above all others, we too, bring our reverence, for you have given birth to the girl from whom He will come Who is the basis of all our hope. Blessed, indeed, above all others, and blessed in your offspring!

The tongues of all believers sing the praises of your child. Every voice is raised in joy at her birth. How worthy Ann is of praise, most worthy, for she received the message of God's goodness, and brought forth such fruit that from it would come Our Lord, Jesus.

ST. JOHN DAMASCENE:

Second Sermon on the "Sleep" of the Blessed Virgin Mary

Today that sacred and living Ark of the living God, in whose womb was conceived the Creator, rests in the temple of the Lord, a temple not built by hands. David, her father, leaps for joy, and even the angels join him in exultation.

On this feast day the Archangels celebrate, the Virtues glorify God, the Principalities exult and are joined in praise by the Powers. The Dominations rejoice and the Thrones cannot restrain their happiness. Cherubim and Seraphim proclaim her glory.

Today the Eden of the new Adam receives that living Paradise in which the condemnation of old was dissolved, in whom was planted the Tree of Life, through whom our nakedness was covered.

Today that Immaculate Virgin, in whom there is no spot of earthly taint, but only the love of heavenly delights, today she returns not to dust but she is brought into the mansions of Heaven—she, herself, a living Heaven! From her the source of all life was given to mankind. How then could she ever taste death?

She yielded to that law decreed by Him whom she had borne. As a daughter of Adam she submitted to that ancient law, for her Son, Who is Life itself, had not refused it. However, as the Mother of the Living God she was rightfully brought up to Him.

Eve, who had assented to the seduction of the serpent, was condemned to the pains of childbirth and the sentence of death, as well as being detained below. But this blessed woman had listened to the Word of God, had been filled with the Holy Spirit, had agreed to the message of the archangel, and had brought forth the Son of God without sensual pleasure or male seed.

She was totally consecrated to God. How could she possibly feel the pains of childbirth, or know death and corruption, or be detained below? In her body she had carried Life. How definite, how direct, how certain her way to Heaven! "Where I am," says the Life and Truth which is Christ, "there shall my servant be." How much more so, then, that His Mother should be joined to Him.

ST. EPIPHANIUS:

Sermon on the praises of the Virgin

King David came from the root of Jesse; from the tribe of King David came this holy Virgin. Holy, I repeat, and the daughter of holy parents, Joachim and Ann. In their lifetime they pleased God, and they brought forth a daughter, the holy Virgin Mary, who was both the temple and the Mother of God.

Joachim, Ann, and Mary—these three plainly offered to God the sacrifice of praise. The name Joachim means "Preparation for the Lord," and he did prepare the Virgin who would be the temple of the Lord.

The name Ann means "Grace" and Joachim and Ann certainly received a great grace that they should be chosen to give birth to this holy Virgin. God listened to their prayers, Joachim on the mountainside and Ann in her garden, and granted their petition abundantly!

ST. PETER CANISIUS:

Sermon on the Virgin Mother of God

Why did St. John Damascene and St. Athanasius and the others who followed them call the Virgin Mary by the title "Queen"? They recognized the tremendous praise heaped on her in the Scriptures. She is singled out as having a king for her father, the noble David, and the King of Kings and Lord of Lords for her Son, whose reign will never end.

Moreover, to agree with these great saints, she is the Queen of all the elect in the kingdom of Christ, the great King. This Queen is second to none of the elect who reign with Christ as co-heirs. She is far superior to all the angels and all the saints.

There is not one who excels her in dignity, beauty, or holiness. Only Mary and God the Father have the Son in common. Only the Holy Trinity is above her; all others are below her in dignity and glory.

Wisely the great Athanasius says, "Not only is Mary the Mother of God, she is also Queen and Mistress, strictly speaking, since Christ, God and Lord, Who was born of her, remains always the King."

The Psalmist speaks of this when he says, "The Queen sits at His right hand, robed in gold." Not only is Mary in Heaven, but she is the Queen of the Heavens, the Mother of the King of Angels, the King of the Heavens, His lover and bride.

Therefore, most august Queen, the one and same most faithful Mother Mary, who no one implores without answer, whom every mortal remembers as the bestower of all gifts, I humbly beg, I reverently beseech, that you will present the service of my words at the all-powerful throne of your Son.

F. Nagni

He is born of a woman, but in such a way that the flower of her virginity is not harmed in any way by motherhood.

St. Bernard

Chapter 3

Blessed Is the Fruit of Your Womb

Now it came to pass in those
days, that a decree went forth
from Caesar Augustus that a
census of the whole world should
be taken. This first census took
place while Cyrinus was governor
of Syria. And all were going, each
to his own town, to register.
And Joseph also went from
Galilee out of the town of
Nazareth into Judea to the town
David, which is called
Bethlehem—because he was
of the house and family of
David—to register, together with
Mary his espoused wife, who
was with child.
And it came to pass while they
were there, that the days for
her to be delivered were
fulfilled. And she brought forth
her first-born son.

Luke 2:1-7.

With stark simplicity and almost naked drama, the Gospel tells the history of events at the fullness of time. It is startling in its matter-of-fact style. Almost brusque!

And it is useless to say that there is no way to improve upon it, because Christian antiquity immediately wanted to know more and more. The Middle Ages tried to probe even deeper, and we ourselves have not stopped the search. Nor will future ages.

How is it possible to love and serve the Christ unless He is known? We feel urged to delve into every facet of His life so that we can know Him better, more personally, more intimately. With St. Bernard, we want Him to live again in our minds, our imaginations, our hearts and our actions.

Since the Holy Mother of God is a central figure in the Incarnation, to see her Son through her eyes, to re-live the events as she may have reacted to them, will give us a new insight into the drama of our redemption. Daring as it may appear, we try to enter into the sentiments of her Immaculate Heart as she lived with, and in, Christ.

This is what the Fathers tried to do for their people in their preaching and writings, particularly on the Nativity. They speculate on stern dogmatic truths; they investigate every person and detail involved in the first Christmas; but, over and over again, they turn their attention back to the Virgin Mother. The actions of the weeks before and after Christ's birth are examined, but always, Mary is present.

ST. LEO:

Seventh Sermon on the Nativity of Our Lord

The man who rejoices in today's feast, dearly beloved, is a man of true devotion and reverence, with no false notions of the Incarnation of the Lord or of the Deity. It would be equally false to deny that Christ has a truly human nature, like ours, as it would be to deny that He is equal in glory to the Father.

When we attempt to understand the mystery of the Nativity of Christ, Who was born of a Virgin Mother, the mists of earthly reason must be banished and the smoke of mundane wisdom must be swept from eyes illuminated by faith.

We believe on divine authority. We follow a divine doctrine. Whether we are moved to believe the testimony of the Law, the words of the Prophet, or the message of the Gospel, John, guided by the Holy Spirit, enunciates the great truth:

"In the beginning was the Word, and the Word was with God, and the Word was God. He was with God from the very beginning. All creatures were made by Him, and without Him nothing was created."

And the same teacher continues with another great truth: "The Word was made flesh and dwelled with us. We have seen His glory, the glory of the only-begotten of the Father."

In both natures, then, it is the same Son of God. He takes our nature but loses nothing that is proper to Himself. He shares our manhood to renew man, but He remains unchangeable in Himself. The Divine Nature that He has in common with His Father suffers no loss of omnipotence, nor does the form of the servant violate the form of God.

The supreme and eternal essence which bowed down to man's low estate for our salvation and which, indeed, takes us up into His love, remained what it was. So, whenever the only-begotten Son of God calls Himself less than the Father, of whom He also says He is His equal, He acknowledges the truth of having both natures in Himself. The inequality proves Him human; the equality proves Him divine.

ST. AUGUSTINE:

Book against the errors of Faustus

These words came from Heaven, ringing above the banks of the River Jordan: "This is My beloved Son in whom I am well pleased." They were repeated on the mountain—not, of course, that He was not the Son of God before this pronouncement.

He took the form of a servant in the womb of the Virgin, even though He has the nature of God. Equal to the Father, He did not think it wrong to claim that equality.

St. Paul, elsewhere, makes the same declaration openly: "When the fullness of time came, God sent His Son, born of a woman, born under the Law, to redeem those subject to the Law, that we might receive the adoption of sons."

Jesus Christ is the Son of God and the Lord of David because of His divinity. He is the son of David from the seed of David, according to His humanity. If this were not so vital to us, St. Paul would not have insisted to Timothy: "Remember this. According to my Gospel, Jesus Christ, of the seed of David, has risen from the dead."

It certainly should bother no follower of the Holy Gospels that Jesus Christ, Who was born of the

Virgin without any intimacies with St. Joseph, is called the Son of David. Matthew the Evangelist traces the lineage of Christ not down to Mary, but down to Joseph.

The person of the husband is to be honored precisely because of the male sex. And Joseph was her husband even though the marriage rights were not used. Matthew says he was called her husband by the angel, and he also tells us that she conceived by the Holy Spirit.

One and the same narrator tells approvingly that Joseph is the husband of Mary, that the Mother of Christ is a Virgin, that Christ is of the seed of David, and that Joseph is in the line of Christ's progenitors from David. What follows from this? That Mary is of the line of David and that she is truly the wife of Joseph in the fitting order of united souls and united affections.

Joseph is listed to give due honor to the male sex which should never be separated from the lines of generation, but even more so, that he would never seem to be separated from the woman to whom he was joined in such affection of soul.

ST. LEO:

Letter 13 to Pulcheria Augusta

The mystery of our redemption, decreed from all eternity, was not fulfilled simply in figure or type. It was necessary to wait until the Holy Spirit overshadowed the Virgin and the power of the Most High God came upon her.

Wisdom must build for herself a house in the most pure womb of the Virgin. Then the Word would become flesh and join in His own Person the nature of God and the nature of man. Then the Creator of time would be born in time. Then the Creator of all creatures would be born for all creatures.

For, unless the new man, made in the likeness of sinful flesh, had taken on our nature, unless He Who is consubstantial with the Father had also become consubstantial with His Mother, unless He Who is alone free from sin had united our nature to Himself, then the whole human race would still be in diabolic captivity.

ST. BERNARD:

First Sermon on the Circumcision

O truly wonderful mystery! The Boy is circumcised and named Jesus. How are these things connected? You would think that circumcision is for those in need of salvation, not for the Savior. You would certainly think it preferable for Him to perform the work of salvation, rather than be the subject of it.

Yet, see how this Mediator between God and man, from the very instant of His birth joins the Divine and the human, the highest and the lowest. He is born of a woman, but in such a way that the flower of her virginity is not harmed in any way by motherhood.

He is wrapped in swaddling clothes, but even in this humble garb, He is praised by angelic voices; He is tucked away in a manger, but a radiant star keeps watch.

The circumcision proves, beyond a shadow of doubt, the fact of His humanity; the Name indicates the majesty of His glory. He was circumcised because He was truly a son of Abraham; He was called Jesus, the Name that is above all names, because He was truly the Son of God.

Unlike those before Him who had the name as a mere title, my Jesus bears His name as the truth which before had been only symbolized. Heaven itself had given Him this name, for the Evangelist says it is the name, "which was used by the angel just before He was conceived in her womb."

Note the depth of this thought. He is called Jesus after His birth by men, but the angel acknowledged this even before His conception. He is the Savior of both angels and men; of men, by reason of the Incarnation; of angels, from the time of their creation.

"The name given Him," writes St. Luke, "was Jesus, which was used by the angel." A deed is proven by the word of two or three witnesses. What had been symbolized by the prophets is now made manifest by the Gospels—the Savior is Incarnate. Although the Christ does not need witnesses, either angelic or human, yet for the sake of the elect these are called. Chief among these witnesses are three—the angel, the Virgin Mother, and the virtuous Joseph.

Of this Child it had been written, "From the top of His head to the very soles of His feet, there is no beauty left." That He submitted to the knife eight days after His birth was merely to point toward the crucifixion which, thirty years later, would be the complete fulfillment of the prophecy.

We, too, brethren, must be circumcised if we are to be worthy of the name of our Savior. No longer is it necessary that we be circumcised in the flesh for the cleansing of one member of the body. We must be circumcised in spirit and truth for the cleansing of the whole body. The cleansing of the whole man is effected in Baptism; then it is necessary that we grow as men, in virtue, to full perfection.

Christ gave us the example of virtue in this action, particularly humility and obedience. Christ had no need of circumcision since it was impossible that He commit or inherit sin. As He grew to manhood, it was evident that He neither could nor did commit sin. It is even more evident that He could not contract sin from His Eternal Father or His most pure Mother. Yet the Boy was circumcised, a most pure Lamb, without spot. We must blush, indeed, if we do not learn from such example!

ST. LEO:

Second Sermon on the Epiphany

Rejoice in the Lord, dearly beloved, again I say rejoice. Only a short time has passed since the Nativity of Christ, and already the festival is kept everywhere in the world. The Son of the Virgin is acknowledged throughout the world!

The Word was made flesh in such a way and at such a time that He was manifest to those who believed and hidden from those who persecuted. Still, the heavens themselves declared the glory of God and the news of this truth was spread.

The angelic host announced the birth of the Savior to the shepherds. The star brought the Magi to adore Him, that the birth of the Lord might shine forth from the rising of the sun 'til its setting, that the kingdoms of the East might learn from the Magi the great truths of faith that would spread through the Roman Empire.

Even the cruelty of Herod, who sought to destroy the new King, served this new dispensation. When the cruel king tried to destroy the Child by the merciless slaughter of the Holy Innocents, wherever the terrible news was reported, the heavenly message in the background was pointed up. To make this savage tale intelligible, heavenly signs and the reason for the king's hatred had to be listed.

The Savior was taken to Egypt where a nation still hardened in superstition might be touched by the nearness of Grace. Although they had not cast off the darkness of idolatry, they might yet receive Truth as a guest.

In the adoration of the Magi, dearly beloved, let us acknowledge the first fruits of our vocation to believe. In their joyful service let us celebrate our call to hope. From this day on, we begin to enter our eternal inheritance and to understand the Holy Scriptures when they refer to Christ.

The truth which the Jews blindly rejected pours its light on all nations. Let us, then, honor that most holy day on which the Author of our salvation appeared. The Infant whom the Magi adored in the crib and worshipped at His Mother's breast, let us also adore as omnipotent in Heaven. Even as they offered the Lord mystical gifts from their treasures, let us offer mystical gifts from our hearts, gifts worthy of God.

F. *Nagni*

The Son of the Virgin is acknowledged throughout the world!

St. Leo

ST. JOHN CHRYSOSTOM:

Eighth Homily on Matthew

The Magi entered the house and saw the Child with His Mother. They prostrated in adoration and then opened their packs and offered Him gifts, gold, frankincense and myrrh.

What led them to adore the Child? Certainly the Virgin did not reveal anything, nor was the home so palatial or anything in it so outstanding, that they should be induced to give adoration. Yet they did adore, and they gave costly gifts, symbolic gifts, suitable for offering to God, rather than to a mere man.

For frankincense and myrrh, particularly, are symbolic of the worship of God. Why did they do this? For the same reasons that impelled them to leave home and undertake the difficult journey, namely, the star and the divine illumination of their minds, which little by little perfected their ideas.

This is obvious, since the humble appearances would never have brought forth such a demonstration of honor. Nothing especially noteworthy appeared to their senses: a manger, a tiny home, an unassuming Mother.

Looked at this way, you will get the direct approach of the Magi. They saw Him, not as a mere human being, but as God, their Benefactor. They were in no way deceived by externals, so they adored Him and gave gifts. This is so very direct, and a much different attitude from the indifference of the Jews. The Magi did not sacrifice sheep and calves. They offered gifts which Christians might imitate: knowledge, obedience and love.

And, having received a message in their dreams not to return to Herod, they left for their own country by a different route. To me, this is further evidence of their deep faith. They were not upset or disturbed, but they were quietly obedient.

They didn't talk it over, with words like, "If this Child is so great and so powerful, why must we sneak off secretly? We came publicly and even stood in the presence of the king. Why does the angel make us run off like fugitives?" They didn't say anything like that, or even think it.

This is one of the greatest examples of faith. They didn't ask for reasons; they simply obeyed.

Thirteenth Sermon for the Season

Once it was foretold, "The Mother of Sion says, 'A Man shall be made man in her and the Most High God, Himself, shall establish her.' " O omnipotence being born! O magnificence of heaven descending to earth!

While still being carried in the womb, He is saluted by John the Baptist, still in his mother's womb. Presented in the Temple, He is acknowledged by Simeon, an old man who was well-known, aged, proved, crowned. Simeon first recognized Him, then adored Him, and then exclaimed, "Now dismiss your servant in peace, O Lord, for I have seen your gift of salvation, personally."

Simeon's exit from the world was delayed so that he might see Him born Who had founded the world. The ancient one knew the Infant; in this Child he became a child again. Filled as he was with faith, he was renewed in his old age.

Simeon, the old man, carries the infant Christ; Christ the infant rules the old man, Simeon. He had been told by the Lord that he would not taste death until he had seen Christ, the Lord, born. Christ was born, and the desire, so old in this man's yearning, is fulfilled in his old age. He Who found a world growing old comes to an old man.

Simeon did not desire to stay long in this world. He desired to see Christ come into the world, chanting with the prophet the words, "Show us your mercy, O Lord, and grant us your salvation." And finally, that it may be evident that his happiness is full, he concludes with "Now dismiss your servant in peace, for I have seen your gift of salvation, personally."

The prophets joyfully foretold that the Creator of Heaven and earth would some day be on the earth with man. The angel announced that the Creator of body and soul would come in His own body. John, from the womb, saluted the Savior in Mary's womb. Simeon, the old man, acknowledged God, the Infant.

ST. AMBROSE:

Second Book of Commentaries on Luke

And there was a just man in Jerusalem, named Simeon, devoutly awaiting the consolation of Israel. Testimony to the birth of the Lord is given not only by angels, prophets and shepherds, but also by just men and elders. All ages and both sexes, as well as miraculous events, strengthen our faith.

A Virgin conceives and a sterile woman is found with child. Elizabeth prophesies and her mute husband speaks. The Magi adore and a closed womb sends an exultant greeting. A widow acknowledges and a just man recognizes.

He is well called a just man who does not seek his own, but rather his people's consolation. For himself, he desires that the chains that bind him to the flesh be dissolved, yet, while waiting, he longs to see the promise fulfilled. He knows how blessed are the eyes that will see Him.

He received Him in his embrace and, blessing God, he said, "Now dismiss your servant in peace, O Lord, according to your word." See, here, a just man imprisoned in the body, but desiring to be released that he may be with Christ. He knows that it is a great favor to be released from this life in order to be with Christ.

Let anyone who wishes to share this favor come to the Temple, come to Jerusalem, await Christ the Lord, receive the Word of God in his arms, and embrace Him by good works, as the strong arms of faith. Then he, too, will be dismissed, not that he will never see death, but because he has seen Life.

See how Grace has been poured out copiously at the birth of Our Lord. Prophecy is given to just men, withheld from the unbelieving. Simeon foretells that the Lord Jesus Christ has come for the raising up, or the ruin, of many men, and that the merits of the just and of the wicked will be thoroughly scrutinized. According to the quality of our works, this Judge, just and true, will decide.

ST. ALBERT THE GREAT:

Homily on Luke

He entered the synagogue on the Sabbath, and immediately He was the center of attention. All eyes turned on Him, some with devotion, some with curiosity, and some, indeed, to watch Him and try to trap Him.

The scribes and pharisees said to those who were beginning to admire Him, "Why, isn't this just the son of Joseph?" Note the implied sneer in the way it is phrased.

Both St. Matthew and St. Mark tell us more about this incident than does St. Luke. "Is this not the son of that day-laborer?" or "Isn't he just a common laborer, the son of Mary?" These were the phrases they used, looking down on Him.

We are told that St. Joseph was a carpenter, that he earned his bread by the skillful use of his hands, not eating the bread of leisure and delight, as the scribes and pharisees did. Mary also was the busy housewife, a worker.

This, then, is the meaning of the sneer. "How could a man of such poor, ignoble birth, be Christ the Lord, God's Anointed? This poor rustic can't be believed for a minute!"

But Our Lord was a worker. As the prophet had written, "You have made the dawn, and the sun." We see the same sort of sneer recorded in the Book of Kings, "What about this son of Cis? Is Saul now to be numbered among the prophets?" Bitter sarcasm can be expressed by just a few cutting words!

However, Our Lord answers, "Isn't it true, no one is accepted as a prophet in his own land." Here, Our Lord calls Himself a Prophet. Having within Himself all the fullness of divinity, He did not need sudden flashes of inspiration. But He speaks of His own land as the place where He was conceived and nourished. And, when He came unto His own, He was not accepted.

F. Nagni

Who is holier than she? Not prophets, not apostles, not martyrs, not patriarchs. No, not angels, Thrones, Dominations, Seraphim nor Cherubim. . . . She is the handmaiden and the Mother of God.

St. John Chrysostom

Chapter 4

Holy Mary, Mother of God

Now it came to pass as he was saying these things, that a certain woman from the crowd lifted up her voice and said to him, "Blessed is the womb that bore thee, and the breasts that nursed thee."

But he said, "Rather blessed are they who hear the word of God and keep it."

Luke 11:27-28.

The Son of Mary graciously takes up the praise given to His Mother and delicately, promptly, raises it to a higher plane. No matter how close and satisfying the Mother-Son relationship may be, mere physical maternity is only the starting-point between Jesus and Mary.

Mary's closeness to Christ is a spiritual union of the most tremendous, awesome, love and faith that God can cause in, and receive from, one of His creatures. It actually started long before the Annunciation because of Mary's growing spiritual life in all the preceding years. And on God's side, was His love of Mary not "From the very beginning and before the ages began"? "Before the Heavens were established in their due course," did not God know and love Mary?

That is why the Fathers and Doctors of the Church consider that Mary first conceived Christ in her heart and soul, and then, only later, by the mysterious workings of the Holy Spirit was He accepted into Her womb. Mary heard and kept and acted upon the word of God beyond the capabilities of any other creature. She is more blessed in this than in her mere physical maternity.

We cannot imitate the Divine Maternity, but we must imitate the faith and love in Mary's maternal heart. Praise of Mary will always lead to a higher, more sublime, appreciation of her Divine Son, as happened in this event related by St. Luke.

Devotion to Mary is based on the dogma of her Divine Maternity, both physical and spiritual. Both the devotion and the dogma are overflowing with meaning–they emphasize and glorify the Divinity of Christ. Both cry out the exultant message–Christ is God!

This is the only reason for our extravagant love of Mary. And we are certainly in good company when we praise her. We join with the Patriarchs and Prophets, the Angels, the Shepherds and the Magi. We enter the company of the Saints of every Christian century.

ST. JOHN DAMASCENE:

Third Homily on the Nativity of the Blessed Mother

Matthew starts his volume with, "The Book of the Generation of Jesus Christ, son of David, son of Abraham," and he continues on down to the spouse of the Virgin. Luke, however, goes about it in a different manner.

After describing the proclamation of the Savior at the Baptism in the Jordan, he writes, "Jesus was in His early thirties, being, as was supposed, the son of Joseph, the son of Heli, the son of Mathat," and so on up, even to Seth, the son of Adam, who came from God.

By tracing Joseph's lineage in this way, he also demonstrates that Mary, the Mother of God, is from the same line. The Mosaic Law forbade marriage between tribes, to protect hereditary land rights.

There were good reasons to keep the real origin of Christ hidden for a while and to have Joseph take the place of a father, and even to be called by that great title. Legal standing was taken from the paternal line, and this was provided for by Joseph.

This explains the concern of the Evangelists over Joseph's genealogy. If this had been omitted, or if the maternal ancestry had been traced, it would have been contrary to Scriptural usage, and it would have been considered very unseemly in the popular mind. It was also important to show Joseph's descent from David, and in this way it confirmed the Davidic origin of Mary.

Joseph was a just man. There is unanimous consent to this simple statement. It would certainly be repugnant to this just man to break the Law and marry outside his tribe. Therefore, if he is of the tribe of Juda and the house of David, must not the consent be equally unanimous about Mary's origin? This, then, is the reason for giving Joseph's genealogy.

As the Apostle says, "The husband is the head of the wife." What is true of the origin of the head is true of the whole body. I think it is abundantly clear that the Evangelists take such great care to relate Joseph's descent simply to inform us that Mary is of the family of David, the Virgin from whom, by an outstanding miracle, was born Christ the Lord, before all the ages, the Son of God.

ST. EPIPHANIUS:

Sermon on the praises of the Mother of God

What shall I tell, or what proclaim, about the excellence of the Holy Virgin? God alone excepted, she is superior to all beings. By nature she is more beautiful than Cherubim and Seraphim and all the angelic hosts. Not all the voices of Heaven and earth can praise her sufficiently, not even angelic voices.

O Blessed Virgin, pure dove and heavenly spouse, Mary, Heaven, tabernacle and throne of divinity, you have Christ, the blazing sun of Heaven and earth. Brilliant cloud, you have brought Christ down like glowing lightning upon the earth.

Hail, full of Grace, gate of heaven, of whom the prophet sings openly in his Canticle, "An enclosed garden is my sister, my spouse, an enclosed garden, a sealed fountain."

The Immaculate Virgin brings forth Christ, the living rose. O Holy Mother, immaculate lamb, you have brought forth the Incarnate Lamb of God, Christ. The angels themselves are lost in wonder at this most holy Virgin.

O wondrous sign in Heaven: a woman clothed with the sun, carrying the Light in her arms. This

Virgin is a bridal chamber for the Son of God. The Lord of the angels is the Virgin's Infant.

The angels accused Eve. Now they sing the glories of Mary who has raised up Eve and returned the exiled Adam to paradise. She is the mediatrix of Heaven and earth who perfects the union naturally.

The grace of the Holy Virgin is immense. For this reason, Gabriel first saluted her, saying, "Hail, full of Grace." Hail splendor of the Heavens, Virgin adorned with virtues. Hail full of Grace, golden urn holding the heavenly manna, perennial fountain of satisfying sweetness.

Hail most holy and immaculate Mother, giving birth to the Christ Who existed before you. Hail royal purple, clothing the King of Heaven and earth. Hail incomparable book in which is written the Word, the Son of God, for all the world to read!

ST. JOHN CHRYSOSTOM:

from Metaphrasten

The Son of God did not choose for His Mother some rich or wealthy noble, but rather that Blessed Virgin whose soul was so rich in virtue. This blessed woman, Mary, conceived Christ in her womb because she preserved her chastity above all of human nature.

Let us hasten to secure the intercession of this most holy Virgin, the Mother of God. Let all who are virgin place this priceless, beautiful, and incorruptible possession under the protection of the Mother of the Lord.

Dearly beloved, the blessed, ever-virgin Mary is truly a wonder. Who more wonderful than she, more illustrious, has ever been found—or can be found? She, alone, excels heaven and earth.

Who is holier than she? Not prophets, not apostles, not martyrs, not patriarchs. No, not angels, Thrones, Dominations, Seraphim nor Cherubim. No creature, visible or invisible, can be found to excel her. She is the handmaiden and the Mother of God. She is both Virgin and Mother.

She is the Mother of Him Who was begotten of the Father before the beginning of any creature, whom both angels and men acknowledge as the Lord of all.

Do you desire to know how far she excels all the heavenly powers? They assist at the throne of God with fear and trembling, covering their faces; she offers human nature to Him whom she brought forth. Through her we are granted the forgiveness of sin.

Hail, O Mother! Virgin, heaven, throne, glory of our Church, its foundation and ornament. Earnestly pray for us to Jesus, your Son and Our Lord, that through your intercession we may have mercy on the day of judgment. Pray that we may receive all those good things which are reserved for those who love God. Through the grace and favor of Our Lord, Jesus Christ, to whom, with the Father and the Holy Spirit, be power, honor and glory, now and forever. Amen.

F. *Nagni*

Hail, O Mother! Virgin, heaven, throne, glory of our Church, its foundation and ornament.

St. John Chrysostom

ST. LEO:

First Sermon on the Nativity

Dearly beloved: let us rejoice, for today our Savior is born. Sadness would be out of place on the birthday of Life. He has dispelled the sadness of death and brought the promise of eternal happiness. Let no one hesitate to participate with joy.

There is a common cause for joy for everyone, for Our Lord, the conqueror of death, brings the promise of freedom and life to the guilty. The saint may rejoice for his reward draws close; the sinner may rejoice because he is invited to pardon. Let the Gentiles rejoice for they are called to Life.

The Son of God assumed human flesh in the fullness of time, according to the unsearchable ways of the divine counsel, to reconcile mankind to its Author, and to conquer the devil, the inventor of death, in the same nature where once the devil conquered.

In this conflict, entered for us, Our Lord fought with great and wonderful fairness. Although omnipotent, He did not defeat the cruel enemy in the full majesty of His power, but rather in the weakness of our nature. For this struggle, He took on a form and nature exactly like ours, except for sin.

Entirely foreign to this Nativity are the words applied to all mankind, "No one is without stain, not even the infant whose life on earth is but a day." In this singular birth there is no taint of concupiscence, no stain of the law of sin.

A royal Virgin of the line of David is chosen to carry this sacred Child. But, she conceived her Child, the God-man, first in her heart, then in her body. Because she might be afraid to participate in the sublime plan, worked out by the Holy Spirit, an angel was sent to inform her that she would become the Mother of God without any harm to her virginity.

Let us pour out our thanks, dearly beloved, to God the Father, through His Son, in the Holy Spirit, for the great love with which He has loved us and shown mercy to us. When we were dead in sin, He raised us to life in Christ so that we might become new creatures, a re-creation!

Let us put aside the old man, with his works, and take part in Christ, renouncing the works of the flesh. Acknowledge, O Christian, your new dignity.

Never fall back to sinful words or works, for you have been called to a participation in the Divine Nature.

Be mindful of the Head of the body of which you have become a member. Remember that you have been snatched from the power of darkness and elevated to the kingdom of God, the kingdom of Light.

ST. AMBROSE:

Homily on Luke

See how the shepherds hasten along to Bethlehem. It is as if they understood that no one can find Christ in sloth. See how promptly they believe. How could one be slow to believe the Father, Son, and Holy Spirit, the Angels, Prophets and Apostles?

The Scriptures weigh very carefully the force of every single word, so we see the importance of this word, "hasten." They hasten, then, to see the Word, for whoever sees the Lord in the flesh, sees the Word, Who is the Son of God.

Although the shepherds are lowly men, the example of their faith is far from mediocre. How often things that seem lowly to the prudent are more precious to the faithful! The Lord prefers simple folk without pretense or dissimulation, to the company of the learned with their finely turned phrases. The Lord desires honesty; He is not pleased with the pompous.

Do not underestimate the words of these simple shepherds. Even Mary's faith grew through what they said. By their words, the people were gathered together to give honor to God and to marvel at the wonders they narrated.

Mary, however, remembered all these words and meditated upon them in her heart. We may learn from this holy Virgin, not only chastity of word and work, but also the secret of nourishing in our hearts the beautiful facets of our faith.

ST. LEO:

Sixth Sermon on the Nativity

On all the feasts and at all the seasons of the year, dearly beloved, the hearts of the faithful are engaged in meditations on the life of Our Savior, the Son of the Virgin Mother. However, our prayers for help, our words of adoration, our sacrifices and meditations glow with even greater spiritual insights when we directly contemplate God the Son, begotten before all the ages of the Father, and born into human time from a human Mother.

This feast of the Nativity emphasizes the temporal birth of Our Lord. Like a radiant light, this feast brings to our minds the wondrous mysteries of His birth, a marvel both to Heaven and earth.

Not only do we remember, we also seem to see the angel Gabriel presenting his tremendous message to Mary. We gain some insight into the work of the Holy Spirit, so amazingly promised, so wonderfully believed.

Today, the Author of the world comes forth from the virginal womb, and the Creator of nature becomes the Son of one of His creatures. Today, the Word of God becomes visible in the flesh.

Previously invisible to human eyes, He is now carried in human arms. Today, shepherds are taught by angelic visitors that the Savior has taken up the substance of our body and soul.

We are given the form in which we must spread the good news, by echoing the heavenly hosts, "Glory to God in the highest, and on earth peace to men of good will." The very magnificence of the gift demands that we respond to its splendor with reverent awe.

The Apostle teaches us that we have not received the spirit of this world, but the spirit which comes from God, that we may know what God has given us. We worship God in truth by offering back to Him the Gift He has bestowed.

In all the treasury of Divine munificence, what can we find more worthy of this feast than that peace which was first announced by the angels. Peace brings forth children of God, nourishes love, gives birth to unity, and leads to the eternal home of the blessed. It is the mark and character of peace that those who have rejected worldly ambitions are united to God.

ST. BERNARD:

First Homily on the Missus Est

Mary calls Him "Son" Who is the God and Lord of the Angels, saying, "Son, why have you done this to us?" What angel would dare say this! They consider it a rare privilege, being spirits, simply to be His messengers and do His bidding, as David affirms, "He has created spiritual beings to be His messengers."

Mary, recognizing her position as His Mother, did not hesitate to call Him "Son" whom the angels serve in reverence. Nor did God hesitate to respond to the name and to revere the maternal Majesty He had bestowed on her.

A little further on, the Evangelist says, "And He was subject to them." Who was subject to whom? God was subject to man! The God Who commands all the orders of angels was subject to Mary.

Which shall we admire first? The tremendous submission of the Son of God, or the tremendous God-given dignity of the Mother of God? Both are marvels: both amazing.

When God obeys a woman, it is humility without precedent. When a woman commands her God, it is sublime beyond measure. In praising virgins, we read that they follow the Lamb wherever He goes. How can we possibly praise sufficienty the Virgin who leads Him?

Learn, O man, to obey; learn, O earth, to be subject; learn, O dust, to bow down. In speaking of your Creator, the Evangelist says, "He was subject to them." Blush, proud ashes, for God humiliates Himself and you exalt yourself. God submits to men, but you, ignoring His example, seek to dominate your fellow men.

O Blessed Mary! You lack neither humility, nor virginity. And it is a truly remarkable virginity which did not fear, but rather honored, fruitfulness. No less singular is the humility which did not suffer, indeed, was exalted by the fruitful virginity.

Which of these is not marvelous or incomparable? Which one is not singular? The wonder is that we do not stop to contemplate! What is more worthy of admiration, the fruitfulness of the Virgin or the integrity of the Mother; the Divine dignity of the Child or the humility of the Sublime Infant?

Perhaps it is preferable, since each part is so incomparably excellent, each part more inspiring than the last, that the mystery be contemplated as a whole.

We certainly should not be surprised that God, Who is blessed and wonderful in His saints, should be yet more marvelous in His Mother. Virgins may praise the motherhood of this Virgin; the married may honor the virginity of this Mother. All men can imitate the humility of the Mother of God.

ST. BEDE THE VENERABLE:

Homily on Luke

Great is the faith and devotion of this woman, for, while the scribes and pharisees are busy testing and blaspheming the Lord, she alone sincerely acknowledges the Incarnation. She so professes her faith that she refutes the calumnies of those present and the malice of future heretics.

For just as the Jews then blasphemed the work of the Holy Spirit and denied that He, the Son, was consubstantial with the Father, so later heretics denied that He was truly the Son of Mary, consubstantial with His Mother. They denied that by the power of the Holy Spirit, the ever-virgin Mary brought forth the only-begotten Son of God in the flesh.

But, if the flesh of the Son of God Incarnate is not from the flesh of the Virgin Mother, there is no reason to bless the womb that bore Him or the breasts that nursed Him. However, the Apostle distinctly says that God sent His Son into the world, born of a woman, born under the Law.

The distinction that some have tried to make, that He was born of a woman but made under the

Law, is without reason or foundation. He was actually formed in and from the woman's virginal womb. His flesh was not created out of nothing, nor made from some foreign material. He is the flesh and blood of His Mother.

Otherwise, He would not be the Son of Man because He would have had no origin from man. Let us indeed, join the woman of this Gospel passage in her praise. Let us reflect the voice of the Catholic Church when it condemned the heretic Eutyches, and let us sing out above the crowd, "Blessed is the womb that bore You and the breasts that nursed You!"

Blessed indeed is the Mother of whom it has been said, "She has given birth to the King who rules Heaven and earth forever."

"But even more blessed," responds the Savior, "are those who hear the word of God and act on it." He graciously acknowledges her praise. He points out that not only is Mary blessed because she gave Him birth according to the flesh, but that she and all others are blessed who bring Him forth by good works, and nourish Him by their own lives and by sharing their faith with others.

Truly the Mother of God is blessed that she gave Him His flesh, but she is by far the most blessed of all in that her love for Him excels for all eternity.

F. Nagni

She ardently desires that not a single soul perish whom her Son has redeemed by His precious Blood in His saving death.

St. Robert Bellarmine

Chapter 5

Pray for Us, Sinners

Now there were standing by the cross of Jesus his mother and his mother's sister, Mary of Cleophas, and Mary Magdalene. When Jesus, therefore, saw his mother and the disciple standing by, whom he loved, he said to his mother, "Woman, behold, thy son." Then he said to the disciple, "Behold, thy mother." And from that hour the disciple took her into his home.

John 19:25-27.

The Immaculate Heart of Mary was consecrated at the foot of the Cross. In those truly excruciating three hours, her Heart was exercised, widened, deepened until it could love the whole world with a maternal dedication. •

Christian devotion has instinctively responded to this. Like little children, wounded, hurt, tearful, dirty, the Christian heart has always turned to her with the plea, "Mother, pray for us, sinners." That Mary always does gather in her little ones is acknowledged by such phrases as, "Remember, O most gracious Virgin Mary . . . never was it known . . . that anyone who asked your help . . . was left unaided!"

The ways in which Mary comes to our aid are as many and as varied as a mother's love and ingenuity can devise. Maybe she speaks for us at the throne of Grace, for who can approach with more confidence than she? Maybe she goes hand in hand with us to present us to her Son, for who is more acceptable in His presence than she?

By meditating on her life, we can apply the perfect example of Christ-likeness to our own lives. Her very being is an answer to our prayers.

Catholic Action, with its magnificent zeal for social justice and charity, with its tremendous apostolate to bring Christ to the souls in the market-place, runs the risk of the desperate heresy of good works alone, unless it finds its inspiration in union with God, in personal love of Christ. The Fathers and Doctors of the Church, in ringing, living tones, proclaim—The most direct way into the Heart of Christ is through His Mother!

ST. PETER DAMIAN:

Homily on the Nativity of the Blessed Virgin Mary

O Virgin Mother of God, more beautiful than the sun and the moon, come, O Lady, and lift up those who bring their supplications. "Return, return, O Sunamitess, that we may see you." O great and blessed Lady, turn to our aid in power.

He Who is mighty has done great things for you and has given you all power in Heaven and on earth. Nothing is impossible to you. You can even give hope to the desperate!

How can Power itself refuse you power, when He took His flesh from you. You can approach that golden altar of human reconciliation, not simply to ask, but even to command—no longer a handmaiden, but the Queen.

Your very nature and power move you to act on our behalf, since the more powerful you are, the more merciful you will be. Power is more glorious when it is exercised in forgiveness.

Turn back to us in love. I know, O Lady, that you are most loving, that you love us with an invincible love. In you and through you, your Son and God has loved us with the highest love. Who knows how often you have held back God's anger, when justice was about to go forth from the throne of God?

Turn back to us in your outstanding love. In your hands are all the treasures of divine mercy, and you alone have been chosen to dispense such graces. May your hand never fail when you seek occasion to save the weak or to pour out mercy. Your glory is not diminished, but increased, when sinners receive mercy and the just are taken up in glory.

Turn towards us, O Sunamitess, you who were once poor, whose soul was pierced by a sword, who was called the wife of a carpenter. Turn, that we may behold the highest glory there is, besides God's glory. Turn, that we may cling to you and find a strong protector.

Listen to us, for your Son honors you and refuses you nothing, and He is God, blessed forever. Amen.

ST. ROBERT BELLARMINE:

Homily on the Seven Words

The task that Our Lord gave to St. John of caring for the Virgin Mother was certainly a light burden and a sweet yoke. Who would not joyfully take into his own home the Mother in whose womb the Word lived for nine months, and under whose loving care He lived for thirty years?

Who would not envy this beloved disciple of the Lord, who, when His Lord was gone, was granted the presence of the Mother? And yet, I feel that I can say that we, too, may have her presence granted by our prayers. The most merciful Lord, Who was born for us, and, in His great love, crucified for us, will respond and say to each of us, "Behold, your Mother"; and to her, Behold, each one of these, your sons and daughters."

This most loving Master is not sparing of His graces to those who approach His throne with faith and confidence, with a contrite and humble heart, with sincerity. Since He wishes to make us co-heirs to His entire kingdom, certainly He will not hesitate to make us co-heirs to the love of His Mother.

Nor will this most loving Virgin hesitate to embrace in her maternal love so great a multitude of children. She ardently desires that not a single soul perish whom her Son has redeeemed by His precious Blood in His saving death.

Let us draw near to the throne of Christ's grace with confidence. Let us humbly beg, even with tears, that He will turn to His Mother and say, "Behold, these are your children," and to each and every one of us, "Behold, your Mother, and mine!"

ST. AMBROSE:

Homily on Luke

It is clear to everyone that when faith is demanded, the reason for believing must be shown. Therefore, when the angel announced so mysterious a message to Mary, he immediately gave as proof the news that the elderly, sterile Elizabeth had conceived, "that you may realize that all things are possible with God."

When Mary heard this, she hastened off to the mountain village, not because she was incredulous about the prophecy, uncertain about the messenger, or doubtful about the fact. She went to rejoice in the answer to prayer; she was prepared to help in fraternal charity; she hastened to participate in happiness.

When one is filled with God, it is natural to desire to advance still further. Indeed, the Holy Spirit expects us to make good use of grace.

We can learn to advance in virtue from the example of Mary. See her solicitude for a relative who was with child. Mary's modesty, which previously kept her from much contact with people, did not keep her from undertaking a difficult journey when a work of charity was involved.

When the Virgin knew she was needed, she did not think up excuses or plead the weakness of her sex. She left home immediately and hastened into the mountain country to be of service. Young women, follow this example. Do not waste time in idle visits and public gossip.

Mary left home promptly when needed, and even remained three months in her cousin's service. Learn modesty from Mary, and learn humility. She visits simply as a cousin from some distance, as a junior to a senior. Not only did this noble Virgin come, she was the first to offer a greeting.

Mary knew that virginity and humility go hand in hand. She was willing to defer to others. She is the teacher of humility who is the perfect example of purity. Humility is essential to faith and truth.

Meditate on this. The superior comes to the lesser one; Mary to Elizabeth; Christ to John. Afterwards, too, Christ comes to John to sanctify John's baptismal rite in the River Jordan.

Notice how quickly benefits result from Mary's visit and Christ's presence. Elizabeth first heard Mary's voice, but John first sensed the nearness of grace. Elizabeth heard in the natural order; John exulted in the mysterious order of grace. Elizabeth acknowledges Mary; John responds to Christ.

The two mothers speak words of grace; the two infants communicate on the spiritual plane. As the mothers draw close in fraternal charity, by a two fold miracle, they prophesy in the spirit of their children.

The baby exults and the mother is filled with the Holy Spirit. When the son receives the Holy Spirit first, and only then does his mother receive it, it is through him. Then she cried out, "How wonderful it is that the Mother of my Lord comes to me!" That is: this is a great and unexpected honor that the Mother of the Lord, a woman so singularly chosen, should be coming here to see me. I sense the miracle. I acknowledge the mystery—the Mother of my Lord even now carries the Divine Word within Her.

Mary remained with her for three months and then returned home. Notice that Mary came to help, but she also performed a more mysterious service. It was not merely for friendship that she remained, but also to perfect the prophet, as yet unborn.

If her mere entrance produced such effects that the child leaped in his mother's womb, and the mother herself was filled with the Holy Spirit, how much greater fruit must have been produced by Mary's prolonged presence? It was in this way that the prophet was anointed, and, like a good athlete, he was exercised in his mother's womb for the courageous struggle that was ahead of him.

ST. AUGUSTINE:

Treatise on the Creed for the Catechumens

Holy Mother Church received you in her womb by the most sacred sign of the Cross, even as she received the brethren before you. She gives birth to you, the children-to-be, through the sacred waters of regeneration.

Joyfully, this great Mother brings forth joyful children to the true light of day, having nourished you in her womb with the food of Truth. The children of Eve are brought forth through labor to a life of toil, but not so with this Mother, since she does not labor under the sentence of Eve.

Mother Church loosens the bond of death brought upon the children of disobedience. By her obedience, this Mother is a channel of love and Life. All the sacramental rites now preparing you for Baptism, the prayers and the canticles, the exorcisms and the penances, the humble garments and the prostrations, all of these prepare you for presentation to Christ, happily reborn of Holy Mother Church.

By the sign of the Cross you are protected from the power of the devil during this holy rebirth. In the Apocalypse of St. John the Apostle, we read that the dragon stood by the woman as she gave birth, ready to pounce upon her child. The dragon, of course, is the devil. The woman is the Virgin Mary who, preserving her own virginal integrity, gave birth to the Virgin Head of the Church.

In this, Mary symbolizes the Church. She, a virgin, brought forth a Son. Holy Mother Church, herself a virgin, constantly brings forth children, also remaining a virgin.

Now let your heart be ready, for the devil has been driven forth. In the sight of both God and His angels, not merely of men, you have made this profession of enmity with the evil one. Let it not be only with the voice or the tongue, but rather with every action of your life.

ST. BERNARD:

Second Homily on the Missus Est

"And the Virgin's name was Mary." Let us say a few things about this name, which can be interpreted to mean "Star of the Sea," an apt designation for the Virgin Mother.

She is most beautifully likened to a star, for a star pours forth its light without losing anything of its nature. She gave us her Son without losing anything of her virginity. The glowing rays of a star take nothing away from its beauty. Neither has the Son taken anything away from His Mother's integrity.

She is that noble star of Jacob, illuminating the whole world, penetrating from the highest Heavens to the deepest depths of hell. The warmth of her brilliance shines in the minds of men, encouraging virtue, extinguishing vice. She is that glorious star lighting the way across this vast ocean of life, glowing with merits, guiding by example.

When you find yourself tossed by the raging storms on this great sea of life, far from land, keep your eyes fixed on this Star to avoid disaster. When the winds of temptation or the rocks of tribulation threaten, look up to the Star, call upon Mary!

When the waves of pride or ambition sweep over you, when the tide of detraction or jealousy runs against you, look up to the Star, call upon Mary! When the shipwreck of avarice, anger, or lust seems imminent, call upon Mary!

If the horror of sin overwhelms you and the voice of conscience terrifies you, if the fear of judgment, the abyss of sadness, and the depths of despair clutch at your heart, think of Mary! In dangers, difficulties and doubts, think about Mary, call upon Mary!

Keep her name on your lips, her love in your heart. Imitate her and her powerful intercession will surround you. Following her, you will not stray. Praying to her, you will ward off disaster and despair. Meditate about her and you will not err. Cling to her and you cannot fall.

With her protection, there is nothing to fear. Under her leadership, you will succeed. With her encouragement, all is possible.

And someday, you, yourself, will experience the depth of meaning in St. Luke's phrase, "And the Virgin's name was Mary." With only these few phrases of meditation, we are strengthened in the clarity of her brilliance. How much greater strength we can derive by silent contemplation! In the scintillating light of this Star our fervent service of her Son will glow ever more brilliant.

ST. AUGUSTINE:

Homily on John

Now His hour had come, that hour about which Jesus had mentioned to His Mother when He turned the water into wine, "My hour is not yet come." The hour, then so far distant, had now arrived, when, at the moment of mortal dissolution, He would acknowledge her from whom He had taken mortal flesh.

Then He seemed to hesitate to use His divine power, since she was the Mother of His infirmity, not His divinity. Now, suffering the infirmities of His human nature, He is anxious to provide for her through whom He was made man.

When He commands John to care for His Mother, He teaches us what to do by doing it Himself. As a good teacher, He sets the example, and here, He is teaching that it is the strict duty of children to provide for their parents. The very wood of the Cross, which bore His dying members, becomes the professorial chair, as the Master teaches His servants so valuable a lesson.

St. Paul evidently learned this lesson well, when he says, "If anyone does not take care of his own, especially his family, he has denied the Faith and is worse than an infidel." And what more intimate relationship is there than parents to children and children to parents?

The Divine Master teaches this lesson by His own example. He treats Mary not as a handmaiden whom He had created and was ruling, but as a man caring for the Mother who had given Him life and whom He is about to leave.

ST. BERNARD:

Comment on the Twelve Stars, from the First Sermon on the Virgin Mother of God

The martyrdom of the Virgin, begun in the prophecy of Simeon, reaches its height in the history of the Passion of Our Lord. To the Infant Jesus Simeon had said, "This Child is to be a sign which will be contradicted." To the Mother he had said, "A sword shall pierce your very soul!"

O truly Blessed Mother, the sword has pierced. The only way it could cut was to see the piercing of your Divine Son. After He had breathed His last, when the cruel sword could not touch His Spirit as it passed through His side, surely it pierced your own soul.

His soul was no longer there, but yours did not draw back. Surely it received the wound. We call you more than a martyr because the passion of sense pain was exceeded by the compassion of love.

Were not the words, "Mother, behold your son," another piercing sword? O cruel exchange. John is given to you for Jesus, the servant for the Lord, the disciple for the Master, the Son of Zebedee for the Son of God, a pure man for a true God! How your loving soul must have suffered, if the mere thought of it can rend our hard hearts.

ST. AMBROSE:

Varia

His Mother stood by the Cross. Impervious to the crowd, she stands firm. Despite her natural modesty, the brave soul of the Mother of Jesus endures the public scorn.

Her eyes take in those precious wounds which she knows are the price of redemption for all mankind. She did not back off from this terrible sight, any more than she drew off from the terrible executioners.

As the Son hangs dying on the Cross, the Mother offers herself to the persecutors.

* * *

Mary, the Mother of Our Lord, stood there at the foot of the Cross. We have this on the word of St. John, the Evangelist. The other Evangelists tell us about the earthquake when Christ died, the threatening skies, the darkened sun, the thief's heavenly reward after his holy confession of faith.

John fills in the things that the others passed over, especially that He called Mary "Mother" from the Cross. John obviously feels that when Christ, the conqueror of death, gives the example of filial love, it is more important than the bestowal of Paradise on a dying thief. If it is an awe-inspiring act to show mercy at such a time, it is yet more wonderful for the Son of God to show such honor to His Mother.

ST. BERNARD:

First Sermon on the Virgin Mother of God, from the words of the Apocalypse

We read, "Behold a woman clothed in the sun, with the moon under her feet." Let us embrace the feet of this woman, Mary. Let us follow, brethren, in the footsteps of Mary and prostrate ourselves at her feet in most earnest supplication. Let us cling to her and remain until she blesses us, for she is powerful.

As the fleece lies between the dew and the threshing-floor, as the woman is between the sun and the moon, so is Mary constituted a mediatrix between Christ and the Church. No matter how much we marvel at the story of the fleece covered with dew, we should marvel more at this woman clothed with the sun.

However wonderful these figures of speech, the familiarity of Mother and Son is more wonderful. How can so fragile a nature support so burning a love? Moses, too, wondered over the burning bush, but he drew near, with holy curiosity and devout desire, to understand more fully.

We can draw near to penetrate these deep symbols if we take off the sandals of earthly desires and lay aside the garments of worldly thoughts.

"I will go up and look at this great sight," said Moses. It certainly is a great and wonderful sight, worthy of investigation, when a bush is burning brightly with fire but is not consumed. It is a greater vision to see a woman clothed with the sun, yet unharmed.

It is not the nature of a bush to remain impervious to flame; it is not within the power of a woman to draw about herself the sun for a cloak. This is beyond human strength; it is beyond angelic power; it is much more sublime. "The power of the Holy Spirit will overshadow you!" And how well she responded to the Holy Spirit, Who is God.

This Woman is invested with the all-burning, but non-consuming flame of Divine Love. She has done what the Apostle commands, she has "put on the Lord Jesus Christ." O Lady, your Divine Son remains in you, and you in Him; you have clothed Him with flesh, and He has clothed you with grace!

ST. BONAVENTURE:

Sermon on the regal dignity of the Blessed Virgin Mary

The Blessed Virgin Mary is the Mother of the Most High King, conceived in loving acceptance according to the angelic message, "Behold, you will conceive and bring forth a Son."

Take this in conjunction with the other verse, "The Lord will give Him the throne of David, His Father. He will rule over the House of Jacob forever and His reign will never end. It is as if the angel plainly stated, "You will conceive and bear a King for a son, Who will rule in eternal splendor. Through Him, you, the Mother of the King, will reign as a Queen, co-ruler in His eternal splendor."

If it is necessary for a son to honor his mother. then certainly a King must share the royal dignity with his mother. The Virgin Mary has conceived and brought forth Him Who has emblazoned before Him, "King of Kings and Lord of Lords!"

From the instant that she conceived the Son of God, she became the Queen of Heaven and earth. This designation is revealed in the Apocalypse by the words, "A great sign has appeared in the heavens: a woman clothed with the sun, with the moon under her feet, and on her head a crown of twelve stars."

That Mary is Queen and outstanding in her glory, is chanted by the Psalmist in that psalm especially prophetical of Christ and His Virgin Mother. First he says of Christ, "Your throne, O God, exists forever." Then he adds of Our Lady, "The Queen shall sit at your right side." This indicates her outstanding power.

He follows this with the words, "Robed in gold," to express the glorious gift of corporal immortality shown by her Assumption. Never could it happen that the body which enveloped the Word-made-flesh, which was perfectly sanctified on earth, could ever return to dust, to be the food of worms.

Even as it was fitting that Christ would create her immaculate from her very conception, and to give her the greatest fullness of grace, so it was only right that she be granted the crowning glory of her bodily Assumption. The true faith teaches that the Blessed Virgin Mary, glorious of body and soul, sits at the right hand of her Son.

Mary the Queen dispenses grace, as is intimated in the book of Esther, "A little fountain, pouring forth a whole torrent, is turned into laughing rivulets of sunlight." The Virgin Mary is compared to Esther as to a fountain with a twofold use. She pours forth the light and grace of both action and contemplation.

The grace of God, so necessary to heal mankind, is dispensed to us through her. As from an aqueduct, grace flows through Mary. What her Son won by strict right, Mary dispenses as a most merciful Queen, compassionating her needy people.

F. Nagni

If anyone wishes Divine approval, let Mary be imitated . . . In this one Virgin every species of virtue shines forth.

St. Ambrose

Chapter 6

Madonna

And on the third day a
marriage took place at Cana of
Galilee, and the mother of
Jesus was there. Now Jesus
too was invited to the marriage,
and also his disciples.

And the wine having run short,
the mother of Jesus said to
him, "They have no wine." And
Jesus said to her, "What wouldst
thou have me do, woman?
My hour has not yet come."

His mother said to the attendants,
"Do whatever he tells you."
John 2:1-5.

"Do whatever he tells you!" This has been Mary's message to every generation of Christians. It is as if she repeats unendingly that we must listen to the teachings of her Son, adopt them whole-heartedly, and live them to the fullest.

She once brought Christ into the world physically. Now she continues to bring Christ to His Mystical Body. Her mediation brought about the first miracle, but her mediation has never stopped since that day at Cana. Her title of "Mediatrix of All Graces" is assured.

What a privilege it is to be allowed to praise her, to be allowed to battle her enemies! How often that thought occurs in the earlier ages of Christianity. They recognized that her enemies are those who oppose her Son's teachings. They recognized that all heresies fall before her. Why? Because a real understanding of her position as "Mother of God" will necessarily lead to a firmer grasp on the mystery of the Incarnation.

This is true even in our times. The Communists in China have waged bitter war against the Legion of Mary, because devotion to Mary means standing up for the principles of Christ. A living devotion to Mary explicitly proclaims the highest ideals of Christian charity, social justice, and purity. A vital love of Mary has no other end than a dynamic love of Christ.

The beautiful picture of a Madonna sums up all of Mariology—it is always "To Jesus through Mary;" it is always Jesus and Mary!

ST. JEROME:

Commentary on the Prophet Isaias

And a rod shall come forth from the root of Jesse. Up to the beginning of the vision (or the burden of Babylon) which Isaias, the son of Amos, saw, all of this prophecy is about Christ. We shall consider this part by part.

Jewish interpreters understood the rod and the flower of Jesse to be Our Lord, Himself. In the rod they see the power to rule, and in the flower they see His beauty. We, on the other hand, understand the Rod of Jesse to be the Holy Virgin Mary, as yet without fruit, about whom we have read above, "Behold, a Virgin shall conceive and bear a Son." In the flower we see the Lord, Our Savior, as is mentioned in the Canticle of Canticles, "I am the flower of the field, the lily of the valleys."

The Spirit of the Lord shall rest upon this flower which came from the seed or root of Jesse through the Virgin Mary. In Him has dwelt all the fullness of divinity corporally. This is not a type of grace as flourished in the Saints, for as we read in the Hebrew version of the Gospel kept by the Nazarenes, "The whole fullness of the Holy Spirit shall descend on Him."

ST. JOHN DAMASCENE:

First Sermon on the Nativity of the Virgin Mary

Since the Virgin Mother of God was to be born of Ann, nature did not dare anticipate grace, but must wait until this child of grace had been born. It was only right that she be the first-born in grace, who in turn would give birth to the First-born of every creature, He Who was the Creator of all.

O blessed pair, Joachim and Ann! All creation is indebted to you. Through you that greatest of all gifts is offered to the Creator, that pure Mother who alone was worthy of the Creator.

Rejoice Joachim, for from your daughter a Son is given to us and His Name is called the Angel of the great counsel, that is, of the salvation of the world. Let Nestorius cover himself with shame. This Child is God! Therefore, she who gave birth to Him is the Mother of God.

Anyone who does not profess that she is the Mother of God is far removed from God. This teaching is not mine alone, although it is mine, for I received this as a most sacred trust from our father Gregory, the Theologian.

O blessed pair, Joachim and Ann! We acknowledge your great dignity as proven by the Immaculate fruit of your loins. As Christ once said, "By their fruit you will know them." Your lives were pleasing to God and worthy of her from whom He was born. Through the chaste and holy exercise of your marital rights, you brought forth the treasure of virginity.

ST. AUGUSTINE:

Thirteenth Sermon for the Season

Dearly beloved: Our Lord Jesus Christ, Who is the eternal Creator of all things, has today been born of an earthly Mother and become Our Savior. Of His own will He has been born for us in time, that He might lead us to His Father in eternity.

God has become man that man might become God. The Lord of the Angels has today become man, that man might eat the Bread of Angels.

Today that prophecy is fulfilled which states, "Drop down dew, O Heavens, let the clouds rain down the Just One; let the earth open up and bring forth a Savior!" He becomes man Who has, Himself, created all men, in order to save what might otherwise perish.

For in the Book of Psalms mankind confesses, "Before I was brought low, I had sinned." Man sinned and was rightly called "sinner." God becomes man to free mankind from sin.

Man has fallen, but God has descended. Man has fallen miserably, but God has descended mercifully. Man fell through pride, but God descended with grace.

O miracle! O prodigy! My brethren, the very laws of nature are transformed for this Man. God is born! The Virgin conceives without man. The Word of God weds her who does not know man. She is both Virgin and Mother.

She is a mother, but she retains her virginal integrity. She is a virgin, but she has a Son. With unbroken physical integrity she yet bears fruit. He alone is born without sin whom neither male seed nor the powers of concupiscence have conceived. The Virgin's acquiescence has brought Him forth.

ST. BERNARD:

Second Homily on the Missus Est

What sort of a man Joseph was can easily be learned from the position he was deputized to take. He had the title of "Father" in relation to Christ, and, indeed, was believed to be the father by many at the time. His name, also, tells us something of his stature, since "Joseph" means "Increase."

The great patriarch Joseph is a figure of this man. St. Joseph not only inherited his name, but also his firm chastity, tried innocence, and grace. If that Joseph, sold by jealous brethren, was taken to Egypt, this Joseph hastened to Egypt to save Christ from the jealousy of Herod.

The Patriarch, faithful to his master, refused the embraces of the master's wife. St. Joseph, revering his Lady as the Virgin Mother of his Lord, faithfully protected her. The Patriarch was given the grace to understand dreams. St. Joseph was given the grace to participate in Divine mysteries.

The former Joseph gathered and saved the grain for the people; this Joseph received the living Bread Who descends from Heaven, to protect and give It to the whole world. Beyond doubt, this Joseph, who was the husband of the Savior's Mother, was a good and faithful servant.

He is that good and faithful servant whom the Lord has put in charge of His household. His was the privilege of being the support of the Mother, the guardian of the Son, and the most trusted helper in God's great plan for mankind.

The writer adds that he was "of the House of David." How noble a descendant of the regal House of David this Joseph is! Noble by birth, he was even more noble in life. His worth is measured not only by his carnal descent from King David; he was found worthy not only by the sanctity of his life, the strength of his faith, and the extent of his devotion, but rather because the God of his father, King David, found in St. Joseph another man "after His very own Heart."

God granted wisdom to King David so that he could understand deep and mysterious things and could amaze the great men of his day. St. Joseph was chosen to guard the deepest and most sacred mysteries of the very Heart of God. He was to see, and nourish, to love and protect, Him whom many prophets and kings longed to see.

St. Joseph and the Holy Virgin, both descendants of King David, were to see fulfilled the oath which God had sworn to David. Christ, the Regal Descendant, whose throne would never topple, came into the world in this Holy Family.

ST. JEROME:

Commentary on Matthew

Why was Christ born of a Virgin who was married, instead of simply a Virgin? First, that through Joseph's genealogy Mary's might be established. Second, to protect Mary so that she wouldn't be stoned by the Jews as an adultress. Third, that Mary and Her Child might have protection for the flight into Egypt.

Ignatius the Martyr adds a fourth reason. He says that it was done to hide the fact from the devil, who would, of course, suppose that Christ was born of a married woman, not a virgin.

"Before they came together, she was found with child of the Holy Spirit." Joseph was the first to know since he had almost the privileges of a husband and knew all that concerned his future wife. "Before they came together" does not imply that later they fulfilled the marital embrace. Scripture is simply pointing out that they had not.

Since Joseph was a just man, he did not wish that she be harmed, so he wanted to send her away secretly. To marry a sinful woman, according to the Law, is to participate in her crime by knowingly becoming one flesh with her.

How could Joseph be called a just man if he were going to conceal his wife's crime? Here it is not the case at all. This is a testimony to Mary, because Joseph knew her chastity and marveled at the wonderful event that had occurred. He preferred to be silent about a mystery that he did not understand.

ST. JOHN CHRYSOSTOM:

Sermon

The custom in ancient times was for espoused brides to live in the homes of their bridegrooms. Therefore, Mary also lived with her espoused bridegroom. Why did it happen that Mary did not conceive before her espousal? To protect the mystery and to shield the Virgin from evil tongues.

It is evident that Joseph clearly knew that she had conceived of the Holy Spirit, or he never would have kept her in his home, ministered to her needs, and cherished her so. He above all people would have had the right to be jealous, to denounce her, and to send her away in disgrace.

Joseph, being a just man, wanted to send her away secretly so that she would suffer no harm. After saying that the Child was conceived by the Holy Spirit without any sexual intercourse, the Evangelist brings in this new testimony. For, to prevent anyone from saying, "How can you prove her virginity? Whoever saw the like of this, anyway? Some zealous disciple invented this to please the Master"; to prevent this, Joseph's testimony is given.

Joseph confirms all that the Evangelist says by his own life and works. It is as if he says, "If you don't want to accept my words, believe what her husband says and does."

Joseph is called a just man, and this means that he practiced all the virtues, and that, perfectly. Since he was a just man, that is both good and prudent, he thought of sending her away quietly.

The Evangelist tells us how this just man felt before he understood about the mystery, so that we will understand his action after he knew. Indeed, if Mary were the sort of woman upon whom suspicion should be cast, then, not only did she deserve a public dismissal, but the punishment demanded by the Law as well. But Joseph did not even want to denounce her, much less cause her any scorn or punishment.

Joseph is a man of sublime philosophy, far above the tyranny of passion or suspicion. But what Joseph faced was a fact, not a suspicion. Even so, he was a man of such purity of intention and so elevated above worldly judgments that no shadow of suspicion about the Virgin's purity ever crossed his mind.

Although he lived under the Law, his thoughts rose far above the Law. With the coming of grace into the world, we might expect to see more sublime examples of life also coming forth.

ST. AMBROSE:

Letter to Pope Siricius

On the road to hell there may be some who say that Mary was a virgin when she conceived, but not a virgin when she gave birth. Since conception precedes and childbirth follows, how could she preserve her virginity in conception and lose it in parturition?

If these perverse men will not believe the teachings of the priests, let them give ear to the words of Christ, and the voices of the angels, saying, "All things are possible with God." Let them believe the Apostles' Creed which the Roman Church has always preserved inviolate.

Mary listened to the angel. Then she asks, "How shall this be brought about?" never doubting that it would happen. Finally she responds, "Behold the handmaiden of the Lord; be it done to me as you say."

ST. JEROME:

Commentary on Ezechiel

This gate shall be closed, says the prophet, and it will not be opened. Beautiful indeed is that closed gate through which only the Lord God of Israel may enter, the Leader for whom it has been closed.

The Blessed Virgin Mary is that beautiful closed gate. She was a virgin before childbirth, and she remained a virgin after childbirth. To the Virgin an angel said, "The Holy Spirit shall come over you and the power of the Most High God shall overshadow you; the Holy One to be born of you will be called the Son of God." She remained a virgin after He was born. Forever, Mary is a virgin.

Some have falsely claimed that the "brethren of the Lord" mentioned in Scripture are children born to Mary from Joseph. This is definitely wrong to say about the ever-virgin Mary, who is the closed gate that will not be opened.

ST. JEROME:

From the book against Jovinian

Christ was a virgin and His Mother was ever-virgin. Jesus at times passed through closed doors. He also passed through the closed sepulchre which had been newly cut out of the hardest rock, in which no one else was ever placed, before or since.

What wonder that His Mother is a closed garden, a sealed fountain. From this fountain flow rivers of water, says the prophet Joel, to wash away ropes and thorns. The ropes are the sins that hold us down. The thorns are the cares that stifle the growth of the good seed.

Mary is the glorious eastern gate, says Ezechiel, always closed, concealing in herself, revealing from herself, the Holy of Holies. Through her, the Sun of Justice and our High Priest according to the order of Melchisedech, enters and exits at will.

F. *Nagni*

Beautiful indeed is that closed gate through which only the Lord God of Israel may enter, the Leader for whom it has been closed.

St. Jerome

ST. AMBROSE:

On Virginity

Such a woman was Mary that her unique life might well be an example for all. If an author, for instance, pleases us, we approve his work. If anyone wishes Divine approval, let Mary be imitated.

Imagine! In this one Virgin every species of virtue shines forth. The peace of modesty, the triumph of faith, and the service of obedience are there. A virgin in the home, a companion in work, a mother in the Temple!

How many she has helped with purity. How many she has encouraged to virginity. How many she has been able to give to God, saying, "This one has preserved immaculate the couch of my Son, His bridal chamber without spot!"

Need I say anything of her almost supernatural fasts and vigils, practically forgetting nature's demands in her love of God? She slept when necessary; she ate, more to avoid illness than out of desire for tempting foods. How many she has inspired to good works!

ST. PETER CANISIUS:

Homily on Mary, the Virgin Mother of God

The Church joyfully celebrates the feasts of the Mother of God. Spaced throughout the year, they call the faithful to a work eminently worthy of a Christian: honoring that most Blessed Woman, the Mother of Our Lord and God.

Among all the feasts that have been celebrated through the centuries, the Feast of the Assumption is one of the greatest. No other day ever contained such joy and happiness for her, a happiness of both body and soul worthy of our contemplation.

As it has happened before, certainly on this day her body and soul exulted in the Lord, and she could repeat rightfully, "He has regarded the humility of His handmaiden. Behold, from this time on, all generations shall call me blessed. He Who is mighty has done great things to me."

We who love you and your Son, join in praising the wonderful things God has done in you. O truly Blessed Mother, thrice-blessed in the beautiful conclusion by which God has perfected and completed your earthly life.

Blessed, indeed, not only because you have believed, but because you brought forth fruits worthy of that belief. This day you have merited to rejoin Him whom you loved and served with such joy.

Emmanuel entered this world as a stranger, but you received Him into yourself as into a palatial manor. Today you are received by Him into the regal palace of Heaven, to have Him bestow on you the place of honor, worthy of the Mother of such a Solomon.

Happy the day on which so precious a treasure is transferred from the desert of this world to the joy of the eternal city. All the blessed of Heaven rejoice on this exceedingly joyful day.

Happy the day on which the gentle, loving Bride finds that which her soul seeks, receives that which she has prayed for, takes possession finally of all that she has hoped for—the eternal vision of God.

Happy the day on which the most humble of handmaidens is raised to her position as Queen of Heaven and most powerful Mistress of the world. No higher position is possible in Her Son's Kingdom. Her throne is right next to Christ's in glory.

Happy and venerable is the day on which this Queen and Mother is given so powerful and merciful a position that she will ever be our merciful protectress at the throne of the Divine Judge, her Son.

ST. BERNARDINE OF SIENA:

Sermon on the Visitation

What mortal man, unless ordered by Divine command, would dare praise the Mother of God and the Mother of mankind, whom the Father has chosen before all the ages to be ever-virgin, whom the Son found most worthy to be His mother, whom the Holy Spirit prepared, full of every grace?

With what words shall I, a lowly man, express the tremendous love of that virginal heart, when even the tongues of all the angels would not suffice? The Lord has said that the good man brings forth good things from the treasure of the heart, and this saying can also be a treasure.

Among all the human race, who can even be thought of as purer than she who merited to become the Mother of God, who for nine months had God for her Guest in her heart and in her womb? What greater treasure is there than Divine Love Himself, burning in the Heart of this Virgin as in a furnace?

From her Heart, as from a furnace of Divine Love, the Blessed Virgin spoke words of the most ardent love. Since from a vessel of good rich wine only good wine can be poured, and from a burning furnace only great heat can come, so from Mary, Christ can receive only the words of ardent love.

The Mother and Mistress of Wisdom speaks few words, but each is filled with great depths of meaning. We read that the Mother of Christ spoke seven times, seven words filled with wisdom, as if to show, mystically, that she is filled with the sevenfold graces.

Twice she spoke to the angel, and twice to Elizabeth. She also spoke to her Son twice, once in the Temple and once at the marriage feast. There she also spoke to the attendants.

On all these occasions, she spoke very little, except for the one time when the praises of God just poured forth from her lips in thanksgiving. Then she said, "My soul doth magnify the Lord." But note that here she was speaking to God, not to men.

These seven words proceed according to seven orders of love. They are like seven flames of love from the furnace of her Heart.

F. Nagni

The Mother and Mistress of Wisdom speaks few words, but each is filled with great depths of meaning.

St. Bernardine of Siena

F. Nagni

The mother of our race brought punishment to mankind; the Mother of Our Lord brought salvation to mankind.

St. Augustine

Chapter 7

Mutans Hevae Nomen

Now the woman saw that the tree was good for food, pleasing to the eyes, and desirable for the knowledge it would give. She took of its fruit and ate it, and also gave some to her husband and he ate.

Then the Lord God said to the serpent: "Because you have done this, cursed are you among all beasts of the field; on your belly shall you crawl, dust shall you eat, all the days of your life.

"I will put enmity between you and the woman, between your seed and her seed; he shall crush your head, and you shall lie in wait for his heel."

Gen. 3:6, 14-15.

Christ the new Adam! Mary the new Eve! This is a theme which has already appeared in these pages, and it is a familiar idea throughout Christian literature. The medieval writers loved the play on words—Eva, transformed into Ave!

The Proto-Evangelium in the third chapter of Genesis is the first promise of a Savior, and it is made in the presence of Adam and Eve. This Holy Redeemer, the new Adam Who will be the new head of the human race, is brought into the world by the new Eve. Her position as the new mother of the human race is assured.

All that Eve could have been, is found in its fullness in Mary. This was promulgated to the whole world by that glorious AVE! Is it any wonder that we can apply to Mary the glorious phrases, "Who is she that approaches as a brilliant dawn, fair as the moon, bright as the sun, terrible as an army drawn up for battle!"

Is it any wonder that the liturgy of the Church applies the beautiful words of Wisdom to her? "From the beginning and before the world was I created." Or, "Whoever finds me, finds life."

In our private devotions we delight in repeating Ave's and weaving them into the Rosary. We can glory in the Rosary meditations which present the life of the God-man to us as seen, in some way, through the eyes of His Blessed Mother.

If we can participate, even a little, in her love for her Son, if we can share any of her spirit, what a whole new love we can develop for Christ. Through Mary, the new Eve, we can reach a greater understanding of Christ's love for men, and of the great sacrifice through which He, the new Adam, assumed His dominion over the human race. To understand, even a little, Christ's position as the new Adam must inevitably lead to a greater love of our fellow men.

Mary Immaculate, guide us in the service of your Son!

ST. BERNARD:

Second Homily on the Missus Est

Rejoice, O Father Adam, and even more, rejoice and exult, Mother Eve. You, the first parents of all the living, have unfortunately given life to mankind, tainted with sin. But now you can be comforted in your great daughter. O Eve, the shame that you have passed down to all women will now be taken away.

The time has come when a Woman will take away whatever men may have against women. Once, man crudely tried to blame the woman, actually saying, "The woman you gave to me, gave me the fruit of the tree, and I ate it."

Therefore, O Eve, hasten to Mary. O mother, hasten to your daughter. The daughter will answer for the mother, will take away the cloud. She satisfies for both the father and the mother. Man fell once, through a woman; now he is raised up through a woman.

What did you say, Adam? "The woman that you gave me fed me the fruit of the tree." These were malicious words which only increased your guilt. But wisdom conquered malice and still found a way to show mercy, even after you responded improperly to God's questions. In His wisdom, God found a treasury of pardon.

A woman is given for a woman, a prudent virgin for a foolish virgin, a humble girl for a proud one. In place of the fruit of death she offers a taste of life. In place of the bread of bitterness, she gives the fruit of eternal life.

Still those words of malice, Adam, and say gratefully, "Lord, the woman you gave to me has fed me from the tree of life. It is sweeter than honey; it is life-giving!"

For this reason, the angel was sent to the Virgin. O admirable Virgin, most worthy of all honor! O singular woman, venerable above all womankind! You have saved the name of our first parents; you have brought life to the whole race.

Who else could God have meant when He said to the serpent, "I will put enmity between you and the Woman." In case you doubt that it is Mary, God adds, "She shall crush your head."

Mary, alone, has won this victory. She alone crushed the venomous head. She reduced his snares to nothing, whether he attempted the corruption of her body by concupiscence, or the corruption of her mind by pride.

Of what other person did Solomon speak, when he asked, "Who shall discover a valiant women?"

The wise man knew the fragile nature of that sex. But the wise man also knew that God had promised, as was fitting, that the serpent who had conquered through a woman, would himself be conquered by a woman.

That was why he cried out in wonder, "Who shall discover a valiant woman?" It was as if he said, "If our salvation depends on a woman, the restoration of our innocence, our triumph over the enemy, then it must indeed be a remarkable woman whom God will make suitable for the task."

ST. IRENAEUS:

From the Book against Heresies

When the Lord came unto His own, He took upon Himself their nature. He took upon Himself the burden of their sins, that what was lost through the disobedience connected with a tree, He might recapture by His obedience on the tree of the Cross.

The seduction of a fallen angel drew Eve, a virgin soon to be united to her husband, while the glad tidings of the holy angel drew Mary, a Virgin already espoused, to begin the plan which would dissolve the bonds of that first snare. Both were addressed by an angel, but with what different results!

Eve responded by falling away from God. Mary's obedience to the angelic message brought God into her womb. Eve listened and lost God; Mary listened and obeyed God.

The Virgin Mary has become the advocate for the virgin Eve. Death was brought upon the world by a virgin; life has triumphed by the Virgin. Mary's obedience has finally balanced the debt of disobedience.

ST. AUGUSTINE:

Treatise on the Creed for Catechumens

Death came through a woman;
    Life came through a Woman.
Eve brought ruin;
    Mary brought salvation.
Eve was misled by the devil;
    Mary the Virgin, gave birth to the Savior.

Eve freely gave in to the temptation of the serpent, shared it with her man, and both merited death.
    Mary, infused with heavenly grace, brought forth the Life by which mortal flesh is restored to life.

Who is the author of this? The Son of the Virgin and the Spouse of virgins, Who caused the fruitfulness of His Mother without taking anything away from her virginity.

ST. BERNARD:

Homily on St. Mary

To extol the gift of grace and to humiliate human wisdom, God chose to take flesh from a woman, a virgin, to restore like to like, to cure contrary by contrary, to pluck out the painful thorn, to delete the handwriting of sin.

Eve was a thorn, but Mary was a rose. Eve, the thorn, inflicted wounds, but Mary, the rose, soothed all passions. Eve, the thorn, brought death, but Mary, the rose, made salvation accessible.

Mary, the rose, had the glowing whiteness of virginity, the brilliant red of charity. She had purity of body, beauty of soul. The whiteness signifies her pursuit of virtue, her purity of mind, her great love of God. The redness manifests her triumph over vice, her mortification of the flesh, her compassion for her neighbor.

ST. AUGUSTINE:

Eighteenth Sermon on the Saints

Dearly beloved: That long desired day has come, the birthday of the venerable and blessed ever-virgin Mary, on whose feast the whole world rejoices and exults. She is the flower of the field from whom has come that most precious lily of the valley.

At her birth, the nature of our first parents was restored and their guilt destroyed. The unhappy legacy of Eve, "In sorrow shall you bear your children," is ended in Mary, for she gave birth to the Lord in joy.

Eve mourned, but Mary exulted. Eve carried tears in her womb; Mary carried joy. Eve gave birth to a sinner; Mary gave us the Innocent One. The mother of our race brought punishment to mankind; the Mother of Our Lord brought salvation to mankind.

From Eve came sin; from Mary, grace. Eve was the source of death; Mary was the source of Life. One hurt us, the other helped us. The faith and obedience of Mary compensate for the pride and disobedience of Eve.

Now Mary can sing and rejoice in all of her youthful happiness. The joyful choirs of men can join with her in praise. Hear her sing, "My soul praises the Lord and my spirit rejoices in God, my Savior. He has had regard for the humility of His handmaiden. From now on, all generations shall call me blessed. Because He Who is powerful has done great things for me."

The miraculous new birth has conquered the cause of grief. Mary's song of praise quiets the mourning of Eve.

ST. BERNARD:

Sermon on the Apocalypse

We have been seriously harmed by one man and one woman. But, thanks be to God, by one Man and one Woman, all has been restored to us, and indeed, with greater abundance. The gift does not simply equal the crime. The magnificence of the benefits far exceeds the evil deed.

That most prudent and merciful Sculptor did not break up what had been crushed, but He refashioned it in a yet better way. From human flesh He formed a new Adam, and in Mary, He uncovered a new Eve.

Know, O man, the plan of God. Recognize the plan of His wisdom, the counsel of His love. The price of universal salvation has been given us through Mary, that she might retrieve the reputation of our first mother, Eve.

From Eve came that most cruel poison, sin. Through Mary, God has bestowed on us a most merciful antidote. Eve brought seduction; Mary brings propitiation. Eve brought deceit; Mary brings the Truth. Human frailness finds a mediatrix in Mary.

F. Nagni

. . . Therefore we are obliged to say that the Blessed Virgin is the Mother of God, not that she is the Mother of Divinity, but because she is the Mother, according to His human nature, of the Person who has both the Divine and the human nature.

St. Thomas Aquinas

Chapter 8

A Tribute from Thomas

And a great sign appeared in
heaven: a woman clothed
with the sun, and the moon
under her feet, and
upon her head a crown
of twelve stars. And
being with child, she cried out
in her travail and was in
the anguish of delivery.
Apoc. 12:1-2.

The Church labors to bring forth children worthy of God—other-Christs. In this, the Church resembles the ever-virgin Mother of God, who gave Christ to the world. In bringing the source of grace into the world, Mary began the apostolate which she continues to this very day: bringing Christ to mankind.

In this chapter, we will turn to another mode of expression to examine Mary's work. St. Thomas Aquinas turns the incisive light of reason on the great mysteries of Christianity. He is a delight, both in the form he uses, and in the calm, clear, logical, step-by-step patience with which he attacks a problem.

He sets up the objections first, then he treats the Catholic doctrine, and finally he answers the objections. It is the unhurried pace set by the Hound of Heaven, Himself. Francis Thompson would have recognized the offensive position and the method, some of which he captured in his great poem.

Father Walter Farrell did, too, because he captured the spirit of St. Thomas in his work, "The Companion to the Summa." In the spirit of Aquinas, we must acknowledge and join all the Christian ages in paying allegiance to Mary as the Mother of God—simply because it is a dogmatic fact. The lack of emotion and sentiment is tribute enough to a truth which should be clear to everyone!

ST. THOMAS AQUINAS:

SUMMA THEOLOGIAE, Book 3, Question 28, Article 4

Did the Mother of God have a vow of virginity?

It would seem that the Mother of God did not take a vow of virginity. In Deuteronomy we read, "There shall be no one among you sterile, of either sex." Sterility would follow from virginity and so virginity would not be approved by the Old Law. Since the Old Law was in force at the time of Christ's Nativity, the Blessed Virgin would not have vowed virginity.

Furthermore, St. Paul says in I Corinthians, "I do not have any command from the Lord about virgins; I simply give advice." But the counsels of perfection ought to come from Christ, Who is the very purpose of all law, as Paul indicates in Romans. Therefore, it would not have been fitting for the Virgin to vow virginity.

And even further, the gloss of St. Jerome, commenting on I Timothy 5, says, "Those who have vowed virginity must neither marry nor desire to marry." Certainly the Mother of Christ would do nothing reprehensible, so it would seem that she did not vow virginity.

But, on the contrary: St. Augustine says in his book on Holy Virginity, "Mary replied to the Angel at the Annunciation, 'How shall this be brought about since I do not have relations with men?' What she was saying in effect was that she had already vowed her virginity."

As I wrote in the Second Book, my reply is that a work of perfection becomes more perfect when done under vow. Now it is clear that perpetual virginity was an outstanding virtue in the Mother of God. It was fitting that her virginity be consecrated to God by vow.

At that time, the Law insisted that men and women fulfill their duties in propagating the chosen race, so the Mother of God would not have made an absolute vow of virginity before her espousal to Joseph. She had the desire to do so, but she submitted to the Law of God. After her marriage to Joseph according to the customs of the time, they both took the vow of virginity.

My answer to the three objections already stated is this:

1. Since the Law seemed to prohibit anything that would restrict the propagating of the race, the Mother of God would not have made a simple vow without the condition "insofar as it is pleasing to God." When she knew that is was acceptable to

God because of the message of the Annunciation, she made the vow absolutely.

2. The perfect fullness of grace was in Christ, but a fullness of grace preceded Him in His Mother. So also with the counsels of perfection, an effect of God's grace. Their fullness came with Christ, but they were anticipated in His Mother.

3. The Apostle's words refer to those who have vowed absolute chastity. But the Mother of God did not vow absolute chastity before her marriage to Joseph. After the espousal, by mutual consent, they both vowed absolute virginity.

SUMMA THEOLOGIAE, Book 3, Question 30, Article 2

The Angel of the Annunciation

It would seem that an angel should not have been the messenger used to bring the glad tidings to the Blessed Virgin Mary. Dionysius says that the highest orders of angels receive revelations immediately from God. But the Mother of God is exalted above all the angels and so it would seem proper that she receive the message of the Incarnation directly from God.

Furthermore, if the common order were to be observed in this tremendous mystery, whereby divine communications are made to men by angels, and divine truths are communicated to women by men, then it would seem fitting that some man, especially St. Joseph, her husband, would have been chosen to present this divine message.

The Apostle says in I Corinthians 14, "Women should be silent in Church; if they wish to learn more, they should ask their husbands at home." St. Matthew, in his first chapter, shows us that St. Joseph did receive some instructions.

And even further, a person cannot announce what he doesn't know. Even the highest orders of angels did not understand fully the mystery of the Incarnation. Dionysius applies the statement of Isaias to them, "Who is this who comes from Edom?" Therefore, it would seem that no one from the angelic choirs could fittingly be chosen to bring the message.

And finally, greater messengers should be sent to convey greater messages. But the mystery of the Incarnation is the greatest thing ever announced to men by angels, so that we would expect that the greatest angel would be sent. However, we know that Gabriel is not from the highest rank, but from the second lowest choir, the Archangels.

But, on the contrary: St. Luke writes, "The Angel Gabriel was sent by God," etc.

My response is that it is fitting for the angel to announce the mystery of the Incarnation to the Mother of God for three reasons. First, it continued the divinely established order of using angels to bring messages to mankind. Dionysius continues, "The mystery of the love of the Divine Jesus was first made known to the angels. After them and through them, the grace of knowing was transmitted to us. Thus the most excellent Gabriel brought the news to Zachary that he would have a son who would be a prophet. Then he brought to Mary the news of the mysterious conception that would occur in her through the Divine Plan."

Second, the reparation of the wounds of human nature that would be effected by Christ was fittingly announced in this way, as Bede remarks in his homily on the Annunciation, "It was an apt beginning that man's redemption was announced when an angel approached a Virgin who would bring forth a Divine Son. The beginning of man's ruin was caused when the serpent, sent by the devil, successfully tempted the woman to bring forth the wounds of pride."

Third, this was a tribute to the perpetual virginity of the Mother of God. St. Jerome says in a sermon on the Annunciation, "How fitting that an angel be sent to the Virgin! Virginity is always close to the angelic life. Certainly to live in the flesh but not for the flesh is more a heavenly life than an earthly one."

My answer to the four objections already stated is this:

1. The Mother of God is exalted above all the angels because of the dignity of the office for which she was chosen by God. But, while she was living on earth, she was below them. Even Christ, because He took on a passible nature, was "made a little

lower than the angels," as we read in Hebrews 11. Because Christ was both wayfarer and Creator, He did not need angelic instructions. But the Mother of God, while still in this life, did have need of instruction.

2. As St. Augustine says in a work attributed to him, "True knowledge of the Blessed Virgin shows her to be above many of the generalities. She did not have many children nor was she under her husband's domination. She carried the Christ Child in her virginal womb by the power of the Holy Spirit." Therefore it was fitting that she receive the message from an angel before she conceived, and that St. Joseph receive it after the fact.

3. Although the angels knew about the Incarnation, they also had to ask in order to find out more fully the workings of the Divine Plan. As the Abbot Maximus says, "The angels knew the fact of the Incarnation, but the tremendous mysteries of the birth of the Lord were not fully explained–how He could be totally in His Father, totally in the universe, and totally in the Virgin's narrow womb."

4. Some think Gabriel was of the highest order, because Gregory says, "One of the highest angels was chosen because he carried the greatest of messages." But this does not mean he was of the highest choir, but simply higher than the angels, since he

was an archangel. The Church calls him an arch-angel, and Gregory himself says that they are called archangels who announce the most sublime news. We may well surmise that he is the greatest of the archangels. And Gregory continues, "His name agrees with his duties, for Gabriel means 'Strength of God.' The Strength of God announces that the the Lord of Hosts, powerful in battle, is coming."

Summa Theologiae, Book 3, Question 33, Article 1, sed contra

When was Christ conceived?

But, on the contrary: as St. Gregory says, "At the moment the angel announced it, in the instant when the Holy Spirit overshadowed her, in that very moment the Word entered her womb. At that very instant, the Word became flesh."

My reply is based on three considerations. First, there is the local motion of the elements necessary for the conception of Christ within the womb. Second, we must consider the actual formation of His Body, and third, we must consider the growth of His Body until It was ready for birth. The second consideration is the actual question, since the first is preamble and the third is the natural consequence.

The first could not happen in an instant and keep the natural order, which demands a successive movement into place. The third, also, need not be instantaneous, since it is growth from within, naturally, and is performed regularly in time.

But the actual moment in which He took flesh, the moment in which the body was animated, that was instantaneous. We can see two reasons for the instantaneous formation of His Body.

First, there is the power of the infinite agent, the Holy Spirit, through whom the Body of Christ was formed, as we have proved in another article. The greater the power of the agent, the faster it can dispose matter. An infinite agent can dispose matter to its due form in an instant.

Second, we must consider the Person of the Son, whose Body was being formed. It would not be fitting for Him to assume an unformed human body. If some time were passed in conceiving, the whole conception could not be attributed to the Son of God. It is attributed to Him by reason of His assuming a body.

Therefore, in the very instant in which the material came to the place of generation, the Body of Christ was perfectly formed and assumed by Him. In this way, we acknowledge the conception of the Son of God.

With regard to the growth of the Child within the womb, growth is a result of augmentative powers. The formation of the body is caused by the generative power of the father who provides the seed which has a formative power. But the Body of Christ was not formed by male seed, but by the power of the Holy Spirit.

The formation of His Body was such as to be worthy of the operation of the Holy Spirit. But, the growth was the effect of the augmentative powers in Christ's Soul. Since this was of the same species as our souls, it was proper for His Body to grow in the same way as ours does. This is one more proof that He has a truly human nature.

SUMMA THEOLOGIAE, Book 3, Question 35, Article 4

Is Mary the Mother of God?

It would seem that the Blessed Virgin should not be called the Mother of God. In things Divine we should not assert what cannot be found in Holy Scripture, and nowhere in Scripture do we see the title Mother or Parent of God, only Mother of Christ, or Mother of the Infant. Therefore it would seem that the Blessed Virgin is not the Mother of God.

Furthermore, Christ is called God according to the Divine Nature. The Divine Nature did not begin to be because of this Virgin, so we should not call her the Mother of God.

And even more serious, the word "God" is regularly used for the Father, the Son, and the Holy Spirit. If the Blessed Virgin Mary is the Mother of God, it would seem to follow logically that the Blessed Virgin is the Mother of the Father, the Mother of the Son, and the Mother of the Holy Spirit. This is not true, so she should not be called Mother of God in any way.

But, on the contrary: In the works of Cyril, as formally approved by the ecumenical Council of

Ephesus, it is stated, "If anyone does not profess that Emmanuel is truly God, and that for this reason the Holy Virgin is the Mother of God since she gave birth of her own flesh to the Word of God made flesh, let him be anathema!"

My reply is that, as is proved in a previous article, every word that signifies a nature in the concrete can stand for any person having that nature. Since the union which took place in the Incarnation is a personal, or hypostatic, union, as proved above, it is obvious that this word "God" can stand for a Person having a human and a Divine nature.

Whatever belongs to the Divine nature, and whatever belongs to the human nature, can be attributed to the Person. When a word is used to signify something belonging to the divine nature, or when a word is used to signify something belonging to the human nature, it can be attributed to the Person.

To be conceived and to be born are attributed to the Person (Hypostasis) according to the nature conceived and born. Since the human nature was taken by the Divine Person in the very instant of conception, it follows that it can be said in actual truth that God was conceived and born of this Virgin. From this, a woman is called a man's mother, namely that she conceived him and gave birth to him.

Therefore, the Blessed Virgin Mary is truly called the Mother of God.

The only way it could be denied that the Blessed Virgin is the Mother of God is if the humanity itself were the first subject of conception and birth before this man was the Son of God (as the heretic Photinus said); or if the humanity were not assumed into unity of Person (Hypostasis) of the Word of God (as the heretic Nestorius maintained).

Both of these errors have been condemned. Therefore, it is heretical to deny that the Blessed Virgin Mary is the Mother of God.

My answer to the three objections stated at the beginning is:

1. This objection was used by Nestorius, but it is easily solved by saying that even though we do not find it explicitly stated in Holy Scripture that the Blessed Virgin is the Mother of God, we do find it explicitly stated that the Blessed Virgin is the Mother of Jesus (Matt. 1:18) and that Jesus Christ is True God (1 John 5:20). Therefore, it necessarily follows, from the words of Scripture, that Mary is the Mother of God.

Furthermore, we read in the ninth chapter of Romans, "Christ came from the Jews according to the flesh, Who is above all, God blessed forever." The only way He came from the Jews is through the Blessed Virgin. Therefore, He Who is above all things and is God, blessed forever, is truly born of the Blessed Virgin as His Mother.

2. This was another objection of Nestorius, and Cyril refuted it in a letter against Nestorius. He writes, "Just as when a man's soul is born with its own body, they are considered one being; and, should anyone want to say that the mother of the flesh is not also the mother of the soul, he would be saying too much.

"We perceive something very much like this in the generation of Christ. The Word of God was born of the substance of the Father, but because He took flesh, we must necessarily confess that He was born in the flesh from a woman. Therefore we are obliged to say that the Blessed Virgin is the Mother of God, not that she is the Mother of Divinity, but because she is the Mother, according to His human nature, of the Person Who has both the Divine and the human nature."

3. The name "God" is common to all three Persons, but it is sometimes used for the Person of the Father alone, sometimes for the Person of the Son alone, and sometimes for the Person of the Holy Spirit alone. We have proved this elsewhere. When we profess that the Blessed Virgin Mary is the Mother of God, we acknowledge that she is the Mother of the Incarnate Son of God.

SUMMA CONTRA GENTILES, Book 4, Chapter 34

Against Certain Errors about the Incarnation

A man is properly called the son of his mother because he receives his body from her. He does not receive his soul from her, but from something exterior. The Body of This Man has been taken from the Virgin Mother.

Obviously, the Body of This Man is the Body of the natural Son of God, that is, the Word of God. Therefore it is absolutely correct to call the Blessed Virgin "The Mother of the Word of God," and "The Mother of God," even though the God-head or Divinity of the Word was not taken from her. The designation "Son" does not mean that a man has taken his entire being from his mother, but only his body.

St. John says, "The Word was made flesh." He would not have flesh unless He took it from the woman. The Word was made flesh from the woman, namely, the Virgin Mother. Therefore, we can repeat, the Virgin is the Mother of the Word, of God.

St. Paul says in his epistle to the Romans, "Christ, Who is above all things, God blessed forevermore, is a descendant of the Patriarchs according to the flesh." He would not have this carnal descent except for the Virgin. Therefore, He Who is God, Who is above all created things, has His Body from the Virgin. We can rightly call the Virgin the Mother of God Incarnate.

The Apostle also says in his letter to the Galatians, "God sent His own Son, made from a woman . . ." From this we can see how the mission of the Son of God must be understood. He Who has been sent to us is the Son of God, by nature, that is, the Word is God of God, born of a woman.

F. Nagni

Before all ages, in the beginning, he created me, and through all ages I shall not cease to be.

SIRACH 24:9

Chapter 9

Queen of Angels

Before all ages, in the
beginning, he created me, and
through all ages I shall
not cease to be.

Sirach 24:9.

The Virgin foretold by Isaias has conceived and brought forth a Son whom we acknowledge as Emmanuel. In the Angelus we commemorate all that was implied by the prophet, as well as the reality which took place in the fullness of time, sparked by the glorious message of Gabriel.

In the previous chapters, the reaction of Saints, Fathers, Doctors, and Theologians has been presented. Now we turn to a man who is more famous for being listed among the adversaries in theological manuals, than for any of the truly Catholic speculations in which he indulged.

The reactions of Francis Suarez were always stimulating. As with the early medieval writers, he was intrigued with the question of the angels. This can easily be explained because of their interest in abstracting from the material world in order to search for metaphysical truths. Since there is no matter in the angels, a whole world of abstracting was at hand.

It is easy to see the transition of thought from the angels themselves to the Creator of the angels, and to His Mother, the Queen of the angels. The salutation of Gabriel, the resounding AVE!, not only began the drama of man's salvation; it was also the message of loving obedience from all the choirs of angels to their Queen—our Mother!

FRANCIS SUAREZ:

TREATISE ON THE ANGELS, Book 1, Chapter 14, no. 19

Now we must take up the question as to whether men are predestined to take the thrones vacated by the fallen angels. According to the natural order of perfection, man is not able to ascend to the order of the angels, since their natural perfection cannot be changed essentially, nor can man's natural perfection be changed essentially. Man is always just a little bit inferior to the angels, and this is true even of the Word as man.

But, according to the order of glory, man can ascend to angelic rank. Indeed, someone has already been created superior to the angels. The most holy Virgin Mary, for example, is above all the orders of angels. Whether there are others besides her can be neither affirmed nor denied for certain.

If it is true that Lucifer had the most perfect angelic nature, and therefore the highest throne of glory, it is most probable that some human being occupies that place. The writings of the saints of previous ages testify that men will occupy the thrones vacated by the fallen angels and ascend to the glory that would have been preserved for them.

These men, then, will excel the angels in beatitude. This is true not only of the Virgin Mary, but of others. She, however, will excel all of them, and will be higher than all the angelic choirs of glory.

TREATISE ON THE ANGELS, Book 6, Chapter 4, no. 16

With regard to the most excellent Virgin Mary, as the Church herself sings, she is exalted above all the choirs of angels in the heavenly Kingdom. It is certain that among all creatures, no matter how pure, the Blessed Virgin exceeds all in beatitude, even the angels.

Furthermore, it is exceedingly probable that even though she alone is superior to all in essential beatitude, a few of the saints may be equal to the highest orders of angels in perfection. In general, though, we can say that the angels are higher than men.

TREATISE ON THE ANGELS, Book 6, Chapter 5, no. 10

We may further question whether the angels knew the mysteries of grace that concerned the person of the Blessed Virgin Mary. This must be answered in the affirmative.

Since there is no mystery after the Incarnation which is secondary in dignity, worth, wisdom or power to the glory of the most Blessed Virgin, this grace of perfection was not denied the angels. Since the angels were shown the great mystery of Christ as man, they were also shown the mystery of Mary's excellence.

Just as Christ is the Head of the angels, Mary is their Queen and Mistress. In their grades and orders they are also her servants. Just as they always contemplate the Word, they always venerate and love her. It was revealed to them that God would become man; it was equally revealed that He would be the Son of the Virgin.

TREATISE ON THE ANGELS, Book 6, Chapter 10, no. 47

On some solemn and public occasions, even the highest of the angels came down to earth to honor the name of God. One such occasion would be the day on which Christ was born, as Luke relates in his second chapter, "And there was with the angel the multitude of the heavenly host." It is not difficult to believe that this was the whole multitude of angels, or at least the majority of every choir of angels.

Chrysostom says this, when he wrote in his commentary on Psalm Eight, "The duty of the highest choirs, namely the Cherubim and Seraphim, is to celebrate the praises of God assiduously. They appeared, even from these choirs, to announce the Nativity to the vigilant shepherds."

We can easily believe that it was from these choirs that the angels came and comforted Christ after the forty days fast and the temptation. Some think that this is also the case of the angel who came to Christ in the Garden of Gethsemane.

It is certain, from Matthew 25, as Christ Himself said about the Day of Judgment, "When the Son of Man shall come in all His majesty, and all His angels with Him;" then, even the highest choirs of angels will descend with Christ to give glory to His Name, to terrify the wicked, to honor the good, and for all the other reasons mentioned by Chrysostom.

Certainly even the highest angels welcomed Christ on the Day of His Ascension, as they probably did on the Day of His Resurrection as well.

We can believe the same about the Blessed Virgin on the Day of Her Assumption. If it is true (as is piously believed and as the Fathers themselves thought) that Christ Himself came down and assisted in the heavenly ascent of His Mother, certainly the angels did. I hold it for certain that the angels did assist on these occasions, sent by the command and the will of God.

TREATISE ON THE ANGELS, Book 6, Chapter 17, no. 24

Although we know for certain, as proved above, that everyone has his own Guardian Angel, some have a second Guardian Angel to help them in their special duties. This would include Bishops, Kings, and some lesser Princes and Prelates. Notice how, in the Acts, they mistook St. Peter and said, "It is his angel," the special angel deputed to guard him as Pastor of the Church.

The same is true of the other Apostles, as Origen indicates when he says that Angels were used to help them explain their message and to perfect the work of the Gospel. Bishops, Kings, and families, as is commonly believed, have a separate Guardian Angel to help them in their public duties. An angel of lesser rank would be their personal guardian, and an angel of superior rank would be assigned them for public affairs.

Certainly a twofold prudence and wisdom is needed to govern in matters pertaining to the common good; so also a double guardian is needed to help those who govern others. This is true of St. Peter, and, proportionately, of the other Apostles. As

Head of the Church, St. Peter had an angel of very superior rank for his Guardian.

This care of a loving Providence is perfectly in conformity with Divine Wisdom and generosity. This is even true, and in a most special manner, of the most Blessed Virgin, who had two Guardian Angels, one for her private person, and one to help her exercise her duties as the Mother of God.

TREATISE ON THE ANGELS, Book 6, Chapter 21, no. 16

Some of the apparitions and works of Christ included the use of angelic ministers. Thus, the most Blessed Virgin knew who her future Son would be because of the message of Gabriel. After she gave her assent, she would have known by the event that she had conceived, but that He was the Christ, true God and true man, she knew and believed because of the Angel's message.

The same is true in St. Joseph's case who was also granted angelic visitations. Angelic action is more distant in the case of St. John the Baptist. Christ Himself illuminated John who was still within the womb of his exultant mother. Through the mediation of the most Holy Virgin's salutation, Elizabeth was granted knowledge. Christ used His Mother's words as an instrument to enlighten Elizabeth, and through her, St. John. We do not know for certain what angelic ministrations occurred in this case.

After His Resurrection Christ often appeared, not in some image or alien form, but in His own Person. Thus He appeared to His Mother, to the Magdalen, to the Apostles, and to the Disciples.

F. Nagni

Happy the man who obeys me, and happy those who keep my ways, happy the man watching daily at my gates, waiting at my doorposts; for he who finds me finds life and wins favor from the Lord.

PROV. 8:33-35

Chapter 10

The Shepherd's Concern

Happy the man who obeys me,
and happy those who
keep my ways, happy the
man watching daily at my
gates, waiting at my doorposts;
for he who finds me, finds
life and wins favor from the Lord.
Proverbs 8:33-35.

Love of the Blessed Virgin was a spontaneous devotion in the hearts of Christians in pre-Reformation days. The terrible insecurity of the sixteenth century was at the roots of the attack on everything that man held sacred. At first, Catholic theologians did not understand how serious the attacks were, which accounts in part for their slow reaction.

The attaching of theses to Church doors or any other public gathering place was not unusual in collegiate towns and centers. Some of the new "theses" were so clearly opposed to Catholic teaching, that the mere response "innovation" seemed to be answer enough. For 1500 years no Christian had held them; how could they be true now? The Spirit of Truth which Christ had promised to send to His Church forever could not fail or falter. That was the reaction then, and even today, many theological manuals use the word "innovator" to describe a Reformation writer.

St. Charles Borromeo, the moving spirit of the Council of Trent, took the decrees of that Council back to his own Archdiocese, Milan, and vigorously enforced them. The horror of a divided Christendom had now to be faced; the Reformation was no longer merely a quarrel among the monks. Innovators they might be; spiritual disaster had to be counteracted.

In the prayer which the Liturgy addresses to St. Charles, we read that "pastoral solicitude made him glorious." In his heroic concern for the integrity of Christ's teaching, he found time to reassure the faithful that their devotion to Mary was definitely an essential part of Christian living.

ST. CHARLES BORROMEO

Rules for the Oblates of St. Ambrose

Book 3, Chapter 1—Founding the Oblates

The priests and clerics of the Holy Church of Milan, who offer themselves for this special work, are placed under the special patronage of the most holy, ever-virgin Mother of God. She is perpetually interceding for the people of God at her Son's throne in Heaven.

Book 3, Chapter 3—Spiritual Exercises for the Oblates

Every day after Vespers, in their mother church, the Church of the Holy Sepulchre, and in every future house of the Oblates, an antiphon shall be chanted in honor of the most Blessed Virgin, changing according to the liturgical season. Everyone bound to the celebration of the Divine Office will participate in this, as well as all priests, clerics, and laymen present.

Pope Gregory XIII grants the following indulgences to the Oblates:

3. To each one who devoutly invokes the Holy Names of Jesus and Mary at the hour of death: a plenary indulgence,

4. For the devout recitation of the Salve Regina, one hundred days indulgence,

6. Each time the Rosary of the Blessed Virgin Mary is recited, by those who confess at least each Saturday and on the eve of her feasts, an indulgence of one year.

Eleventh Diocesan Synod of the Church of Milan, 1584

Regulations on Parish Churches and Pastors

Concerning paintings and statues. In a principal place in every Church, especially parish churches, a painting, statue, or sculpture of the Blessed Virgin Mary and of the Patron Saint of the Church must be placed.

Regulations on the Divine Office

When the faithful are invited to public prayer, the intentions for which the prayers are offered should always be made known. On Saturday, in every parish, the antiphon Salve Regina, or some

F. *Nagni*

She is perpetually interceding for the people of God at her Son's throne in Heaven.

ST. CHARLES BORROMEO

other hymn to Our Lady, must be recited or sung, according to the decree of the Third Provincial Council.

Ritual for the Ambrosian Rite

ON THE FREQUENT RECEPTION OF HOLY COMMUNION

Pastors shall exhort the faithful to the most salutary practice of frequent reception of Holy Communion. This has been the teaching of the Church since its very beginning. We have it in the unanimous teaching and example of the Fathers and the Saints, in the Roman Catechism, and in the decrees of the ecumenical Council of Trent. It is desirable that the faithful receive Sacramental Holy Communion at every Mass.

Care should be taken that not only the Easter Communion, which is necessary by Church precept, but other major feasts be made days of general Communion. Christmas, Epiphany, Pentecost, and all the greater feasts of the Blessed Virgin Mary are such times.

Fourth Diocesan Synod of the Church of Milan, 1574 Decree 43

For those who live in religious houses, who have charge of them, who found them, and for all who attend them in order to study any subject: reason demands that the study of holiness of life, and spiritual exercises, take first place. By prayer, the students' souls will be helped and their learning will be promoted as well.

Therefore, superiors of these houses, and Spiritual Directors stationed there, are given this serious commission. Every day, the Little Office of the Blessed Virgin is to be recited by those who can read. For those who cannot read, the Rosary of Our Lady is to be recited daily.

Rules for Seminaries

PART 3, CHAPTER 2. SPIRITUAL EXERCISES FOR SEMINARIANS

The daily life of the seminarian will begin with a half-hour meditation, followed by the recitation of Matins and Lauds of the Little Office of Our Lady. Tierce, Sext, and None will be recited after the Sacrifice of the Mass. Vespers and Compline of the same Little Office will be recited after the class hours.

Every day the Corona, or Rosary, will be recited by everyone, privately. If there is time before Mass, it may be recited by all. Even those who are not able to attend the Sacrifice of the Mass (e.g. the sick) will say the Rosary. If the confessor of an individual judges it to be expedient, that seminarian may recite his Rosary meditatively at Mass.

After lunch and dinner, the seminarians will make a visit to the Chapel and recite the Lord's prayer and the Angelic Salutation five times, privately. After the recreation period in the evening, there shall be a fifteen minute examination of conscience. The theme for the next day's meditation may be given.

Membership in a Sodality of Our Lady is encouraged, especially for those in Major Orders.

Postscript

The joy that burst forth from Mary's lips in the Magnificat has poured forth into every Christian heart and is re-echoed on every Christian's lips. Mary is the cause of our joy because she brought Christ into the world, the Christ Who gives meaning to human life.

From Bethlehem to Calvary, from Nazareth to the Resurrection, from earth to Heaven, our lives are surrounded, immersed, infused and transformed because the God-man lived and died for us—poured out His love for us. We are surrounded by the love of His Sacred Heart, immersed in the ocean of His mercy, infused with sanctifying grace, transformed by a share in the Christ-life.

All this came upon the world when an Immaculate Virgin responded with all the generosity of her heart to the angel's AVE! This most admirable Mother continues her mission in the world, bringing all men to her Son even as she brought her Son to all mankind. The Virgin Mother of God longs to share her joy with all men. This is the only reason and the only basis for devotion to Mary.

Living Voices

A Select and Annotated Bibliography

The writings of the Fathers and Doctors of the Church are an inexhaustible treasury of our Catholic culture and way of life. Until quite recently, these writings have been somewhat neglected by the English-speaking world. The investigation of this treasure has stirred up a remarkable interest, but it is only a beginning.

The excerpts in this slim volume are intended as a tribute to the Mother of God. It is also hoped that they might whet the reader's appetite to delve deeper into patristic literature. Here are a few clues!

A. SETS: (English)

1. *Ancient Christian Writers.* Westminster, Md., Newman Press, 1946–This lengthy series of translations is still coming off the press. The standards that were set in the first volume, CLEMENT OF ROME; IGNATIUS OF ANTIOCH were very high, and the volumes that have followed are maintaining the pace.
2. *The Fathers of the Church.* N.Y., Fathers of the Church, Inc., 1946–Started in the same year as the above set, this series has also been appearing regularly. The translations are superb, and each volume, starting with the first, THE APOSTOLIC FATHERS, has kept the highest of literary and theological standards.

B. SETS: (Latin)

1. *Corpus Christianorum.* Turnholt, Brepols, 1957—This is a remarkable publishing venture. When it is complete, it is hoped to have critical editions of the Latin and Greek texts of the Fathers. In a sense, it will be the new Migne, but with much more accurate texts. Seminary, university and college libraries will find it an indispensable tool. (Newman Press is the American distributor)
2. *Thesaurus Mundi.* Turin-Lugano, 1958—Another publishing first deserving the ardent support of Catholic scholars, this set intends to become a library of critical texts from the Middle Ages. Roger Bacon, Gerson, Innocent III are some of the authors already represented. The Mediaeval Academy of America, Cambridge 38, Mass., is the American representative.

C. INDIVIDUAL VOLUMES. The Fathers

1. In general, the only available translations of complete books will be found to be individual volumes of the two sets first mentioned.
2. *St. Augustine.* Many volumes of selections are available, and some of his more famous works have been translated independently. Notable among these is Mr. Frank Sheed's translation of the CONFESSIONS.
3. *St. Bernard.* A revival of interest in his works has brought along some interesting translations of selected sermons, extracts, and letters. His major works are still unavailable, for the most part, in English translation. One volume worthy of note is: James, Bruno Scott, ST. BERNARD OF CLAIRVAUX: SELECTED LETTERS, Chicago, Regnery, 1953.

D. INDIVIDUAL VOLUMES. The Ecclesiastical Doctors, and writers.

1. Except for the Doctors who are also considered as Fathers of the Church, their works are almost completely unavailable in English, besides what is quoted in their biographies (also few in number).
2. *St. Thomas Aquinas.* St. Thomas is an exception to the above. His major works are available, as well as many of his lesser works A notable explanation of the SUMMA is available in Father Walter Farrell's four volume set, COMPANION TO THE SUMMA.
3. *St. Bonaventure.* The St. Anthony Guild press has begun publication of the complete works of St. Bonaventure in a magnificent edition.
4. St. Robert Bellarmine, St. Anthony of Padua and other non-patristic Doctors are almost completely unavailable in English. Other writers, such as Suarez, Cajetan, and John of St. Thomas are almost unknown outside academic circles, and seldom translated.

E. BOOKS ABOUT THE FATHERS

1. Altaner, Berthold, *Patrology,* N.Y., Herder & Herder, 1960.
2. Attwater, Donald, *The Christian Churches of the East,* Milwaukee, Bruce, 1947-48.
3. Cayre, Fulbert, *Spiritual Writers of the Early Church,* N.Y., Hawthorne, 1959.
4. Flood, J. M., *The Mind and Heart of St. Augustine,* Fresno, Calif., Academy Library Guild, 1960.
5. Freemantle, Anne, *A Treasury of Early Christianity,* N.Y., Viking, 1953.
6. Gilson, Etienne, *The Mystical Theology of St. Bernard,* N.Y., Sheed and Ward, 1955.

7. Giordini, Igino, *The Social Message of the Early Church Fathers,* Paterson, N.J., St. Anthony Guild press, 1944.
8. Hoare, Frederick, *The Western Fathers,* N.Y., Sheed and Ward, 1954.
9. Quasten, Johannes, *Patrology,* Westminster, Md., Newman Press, 1950–

Meet the Authors

ST. ALBERT THE GREAT (p. 86)

1206-1280. Albertus Magnus was the pioneer of Scholastic Philosophy, and the teacher of St. Thomas Aquinas. In the Council of Lyons he worked diligently for the reunion of the Eastern Churches. He was a Dominican and a Bishop. His feast is Nov. 15.

ST. AMBROSE (pp. 41, 55, 84, 101, 117, 129, 150, 154)

340-397. First a lawyer, then a governor, Ambrose was named Bishop of Milan while he was still a catechumen. He was instrumental in the conversion of St. Augustine. The incident in which he brought the Emperor Theodosius to repentance is well known. His feast is Dec. 7.

ST. AUGUSTINE (pp. 71, 82, 120, 124, 142, 167, 169)

354-430. The famous Bishop of Hippo was the son of the illustrious St. Monica. He wrote extensively on theological, philosophical, and ascetical subjects. His feast is Aug. 28.

ST. BASIL (p. 58)

329-379. Along with St. Gregory Nazianzen, Basil, the Archbishop of Caesarea, was outstanding in the defense of the Catholic Church against the Arian heresy. He ranks with St. Benedict as a founder of monasticism. His feast is June 14.

ST. BEDE THE VENERABLE (p. 108)

-735. The only English Doctor of the Church, Bede is most famous for his "Ecclesiastical History of the English People," and numerous homilies, frequently quoted. Dante, for instance, was acquainted with his writings and mentions him in his "Divine Comedy." His feast is May 27.

ST. BERNARD OF CLAIRVAUX (pp.32, 39, 48, 52, 74, 105, 122, 126, 131, 144, 163, 168, 171)

1090-1153. It could surprise no one that St. Bernard's writings would appear most frequently in a volume devoted to Our Lady. He has been variously known as the "Troubadour of Mary" and "The last of the Fathers." He was instrumental in the amazing spread of the Cistercian Order. His feast is Aug. 20.

ST. BERNARDINE OF SIENA (p. 158)

-1444. Bernardine was a Franciscan of the Strict Observance. He was a noted preacher and was especially devoted to the Holy Name of Jesus. His feast is May 20.

ST. BONAVENTURE (p. 133)

1221-1274. The Seraphic Doctor and most famous successor to St. Francis of Assisi received his doctorate in theology with St. Thomas Aquinas. He is noted for his writings on mystical theology. His feast is July 14.

ST. CHARLES BORROMEO (chapter 10) (pp. 203-210)

1538-1584. Pope Pius IV created his nephew, Charles Borromeo, a Cardinal when he was in his early twenties. This is one case of nepotism for which we can always be grateful, for it gave us one of the outstanding lights of the Counter-Reformation. St. Charles was one of the first to hold the office we now know as the Cardinal Secretary of State. His feast is Nov. 14.

ST. EPIPHANIUS (pp. 63, 93)

310-403. Origen's inconsistencies were first exposed by Bishop Epiphanius. He was personally acquainted with all of the great writers of his century. His feast is May 12.

ST. GERMANUS (p. 23)

-733. This fighting Patriarch of Constantinople was an unflinching defender of Catholic practices in the fight against Iconoclasm. Most of his voluminous writings have perished. His feast is May 12.

ST. IRENAEUS (p. 166)

-203. Among the very earliest of the Church Fathers, Irenaeus began the development of the theme of Mary as the New Eve. He is famous for his appeal to tradition as the norm of truth, and his list of the Popes as a proof of Apostolic orthodoxy backing up tradition. His feast is June 28.

ST. JEROME (pp. 21, 139, 146, 151, 152)

342-420. The great Scripture scholar, Jerome was also deeply interested in the ascetical life. Almost all of the Vulgate version of the Bible is his work. His feast is Sept. 30.

ST. JOHN CHRYSOSTOM (pp. 80, 95, 148)

347-407. Another in the great line of Patriarchs of Constantinople, John Chrysostom was considered the finest preacher of his time. His feast is Jan. 27.

ST. JOHN DAMASCENE (pp. 57, 59, 61, 91, 140)

-749. John of Damascus is sometimes called the "last of the Greek Fathers." He is as well known for his deep devotion to Mary as he is for his many theological treatises. His feast is Mar. 27.

ST. LEO I (pp. 34, 69, 73, 77, 98, 103)

-461. Surrounded by political and theological quarrels, Leo the Great was a strong Pope during whose long reign the Faith grew and prospered. He had a moving devotion to the doctrine of the of the Incarnation. His feast is April 11.

ST. PETER CANISIUS (pp. 64, 155)

1521-1597. The great traditions of the Society of Jesus as a source of literary and theological brilliance were started, in great part, by Peter Canisius. He is honored as the second "Apostle of Germany." His feast is April 27.

ST. PETER CHRYSOLOGUS (p. 36)

c450. This famous Archbishop of Ravenna was considered the equal of

St. John Chrysostom in preaching ability. His feast is Dec. 4.

ST. PETER DAMIAN (p. 113)
-1072. Before his elevation to the dignity of Cardinal-Bishop of Ostia, Peter Damian had been a Camaldolese hermit. He spent himself in the direct service of the Holy See. His feast is Feb. 23.

ST. ROBERT BELLARMINE (p. 115)
1542-1621. A Jesuit Cardinal, St. Robert was a friend and confidant of all the leading figures of the Counter-Reformation, including men like Galileo and St. Charles Borromeo. His feast is May 13.

ST. SOPHRONIUS (pp. 25, 45)
-638. Sophronius was the Patriarch of Jerusalem when it fell to the Mohammedans. He strongly battled the Christological heresies of his time. His feast is March 11.

–FRANCIS SUAREZ (chapter 9) (pp. 193-201)
1548-1617. One of the most distinguished Jesuit authors of his time, Suarez was associated with the outstanding Universities of his day—Alcala, Coimbra, Salamanca. Famous for his commentaries on the "Summa" of St. Thomas Aquinas, he also produced important and independent contributions to philosophy.

ST. THARASIUS (p. 28)
-806. This little-known Patriarch of Constantinople was wonderful for the

purity and serenity of his own personal life. He was devoted to the ascetical ideal. His feast is Feb. 25.

ST. THOMAS AQUINAS (chapter 8) (pp. 173-191)

1225-1274. Known as the Angelic Doctor, St. Thomas brought glory to the Catholic Church and the Dominican Order by his doctrine, both profound and sublime. He was the pupil of Albertus Magnus. One of his most important contributions to Western civilization is the "christening of Aristotle." The "Summa Theologiæ" is his most famous work. His feast is Mar. 7.

Witness of the Centuries

120?–203	St. Irenaeus
310 –403	St. Epiphanius
329 –379	St. Basil
340?–397	St. Ambrose
342 –420	St. Jerome
347 –407	St. John Chrysostom
354 –430	St. Augustine
c400–461	St. Leo
c400–c450	St. Peter Chrysologus
c575–638	St. Sophronius
660 –733	St. Germanus
675 –735	St. Bede the Venerable
690 –750	St. John Damascene
750 –806	St. Tharasius
990?–1072	St. Peter Damian
1090–1153	St. Bernard of Clairvaux
1206–1280	St. Albert the Great
1221–1274	St. Bonaventure
1225–1274	St. Thomas Aquinas
1381–1444	St. Bernardine of Siena
1521–1597	St. Peter Canisius
1538–1584	St. Charles Borromeo
1542–1621	St. Robert Bellarmine
1548–1617	–Francis Suarez

INDEX

Six terms will not be found in this Index because they appear, or are alluded to, on almost every single page: Holy Trinity; God the Father; God the Son; God the Holy Spirit; Divine Maternity; ever-Virgin Mary.

DAUGHTERS OF ST. PAUL

In Massachusetts
50 St. Paul's Avenue
Jamaica Plain,
Boston 30, *Mass.*
172 Tremont St.,
Boston 11, *Mass.*
381 Dorchester St.
So. Boston 27, *Mass.*
325 Main St.
Fitchburg, Mass.

In New York
78 Fort Place,
Staten Island 1, *N.Y.*
39 Erie St.,
Buffalo 2, *N.Y.*

In Connecticut
202 Fairfield Ave.,
Bridgeport, Conn.

In Ohio
141 West Rayen Ave.,
Youngstown 3, *Ohio*

In Texas
114 East Main Plaza,
San Antonio 5, *Texas*

In California
1570 Fifth Ave.,
San Diego 1, *Calif.*

In Louisiana
86 Bolton Ave.,
Alexandria, La.

In Florida
2700 Biscayne Blvd.
Miami 37, *Florida*

In Canada
8885 Blvd. Lacordaire,
St. Leonard Deport-Maurice,
Montreal, Canada
1063 St. Clair Ave. West,
Toronto, Canada

In England
29 Beauchamp Place,
London, S.W. 3, *England*

In India
Water Field Road Extension,
Plot N. 143,
Bandra, India

In Philippine Islands
No. 326 Lipa City,
Philippine Islands

In Australia
58 Abbotsford Rd.,
Homebush N.S.W., Australia